An Illustrated Treasury of

AFRICAN AMERICAN

Read-Aloud Stories

An Illustrated Treasury of
AFRICAN AMERICAN
Read-Aloud Stories

More Than 40 of the World's Best-Loved
Stories for Parent and Child to Share

EDITED BY SUSAN KANTOR

Illustrations by Christian Clayton, Jan Spivey Gilchrist,
Christy Hale and Michael McCurdy

BLACK DOG
& LEVENTHAL
PUBLISHERS
NEW YORK

Published by
Black Dog & Leventhal Publishers, Inc.
151 West 19th Street
New York, NY 10011

Distributed by
Workman Publishing Company
708 Broadway
New York, NY 10003

Manufactured in Thailand

Cover and interior design by Liz Driesbach

Illustrations
© Christian Clayton (pgs. 19, 43, 67, 76, 94, 100, 105, 122, 142, 157)
© Christy Hale (pgs.14, 24, 46, 70, 84, 125, 130, 140, 155, 169)
© Jan Spivey Gilchrist (pgs. 58, 87, 112, 137)
© Michael McCurdy (pgs. 16, 51, 61, 115, 174, 186, 190)

ISBN: 1-57912-347-3

h g f e d c b a

Library of Congress Cataloging-in-Publication Data available on file.

Contents

FOLK TALES

FRIENDS AND HELPERS

HAWK AND CHICKEN TALES

RABBIT STORIES

LIAR, FOOL, AND TALL TALES

BIOGRAPHY

SLAVERY

AFRICAN-AMERICAN SONGS

Myths and Fables

Anansi Gets What He Deserves

Anansi thought he knew just the trick for making Guinea Fowl
his dinner, but he wound up as hers instead.

Anansi lived in a country that had a queen who was also a witch. She decreed that whoever used the word *five* would fall down dead, because that was her secret name and she didn't want anyone else using it.

Now Brer Anansi was hungry because there was a famine and it was very hard to find any food. But Anansi was also a clever fellow and he had an idea. He made a little house for himself by the side of the river near where everyone came to get water.

And when anyone came to get water, he would call out to them, "I beg you to tell me how many yam hills I have here. I can't count very well." So, one by one he thought they would come up and say, "One, two, three, four, *five*," and they would fall down dead. Then Anansi would store them in his barrel, and that way he would have lots of food during hungry times and also in times of plenty.

In time he got his house built and his yams planted, and along came Guinea Fowl. Anansi said, "Excuse me, miss, please tell me how many yam hills I have here." So Guinea Fowl went and sat on one of those hills and said, "One, two, three, four, and the one I'm sitting on."

Anansi said, "Cho! You can't count right." And Guinea Fowl moved to another hill and said, "One, two, three, four and the one I'm sitting on."

"Cho! You don't count right at all!"

"How do you count, then?" Guinea Fowl said, getting a little annoyed with Anansi.

"This way—one, two, three, four, FIVE!" Anansi fell dead, and Guinea Fowl ate him up.

A Home for Sun and Moon

This myth from Tanganyika shows how an inability to admit a mistake leads to unforseen, and unintended, consequences.

At the beginning of time, Sun and Water both lived on the earth and were the dearest friends. Sun frequently visited where Water lived, and they spent many hours chatting together.

But Water never visited Sun where he lived, and Sun started to wonder why. One day, Sun finally asked his friend: "How come neither you nor your family ever come to pay me a visit? My wife, the Moon, and I would be very happy to offer you our hospitality."

Water smiled and said: "I do apologize for not having visited you, but the fact is that your house is far too small for me and all my relations. I fear that we would drive you and your wife out of doors."

"But we are about to build a new place," said Sun. "Will you come and visit us if it is big enough?"

"It would have to be very large, indeed, for me to come in," explained Water. "My people take up so much space. What if we damaged your belongings?"

Sun thought Water was just making excuses for not visiting him, and his disappointment was noticeable. To make Sun feel better, Water promised to visit him when his new place was ready.

So Sun and Moon started to work on their new home. With the help of many friends, they built an enormous mansion.

When it was completed, Sun said to Water: "Surely you can visit us now for our new place is large enough to hold many, many visitors."

But Water was not convinced. Nevertheless, because a visit meant so much to Sun, Water began moving toward Sun's new home. Through the enormous front doors he flowed, bringing with him thousands of fish, water rats, and even some water snakes. By now the water level was knee deep.

"Do you still want my relatives and me to enter further into your home?" Water asked politely.

"Yes, of course," replied the silly Sun, "bring them all in!"

So Water continued to flow into the new house until finally Sun and Moon were forced to climb onto the roof to keep dry.

"Are you sure you still want my relatives and me to come into your house?" Water asked again.

After insisting for so long that Water come to visit, Sun was too embarrassed to admit that it was not a good idea. Instead, Sun said, "Yes, of course. I want everyone in. Bring everyone in."

Finally, Water rose to the very top of the roof, forcing Sun and Moon up into the sky where they have remained ever since.

The Spirit Tree

In Africa, angels are good spirits who come to earth, appearing in any shape or form, to help ease human suffering. Often, they are the spirit of a kind relative who has died but who still wants to help loved ones left on earth.

There was a sweet and gentle girl in Zaire whose mother had died. Her father then married a woman he thought was kind to his daughter, but he was rarely at home and so did not know how cruel the woman really was. The stepmother did not give the girl enough food, so the hungry child often sat weeping on her mother's grave.

One morning, a beautiful tree had grown up from the grave. It was laden with the most delicious fruit, providing the girl with as much food as she wanted. But the wicked stepmother had the tree cut down.

Once again, the girl did not have enough to eat, and again she cried upon her mother's grave. Soon, she saw a fabulous pumpkin growing from the earth which completely satisfied her hunger. A new pumpkin appeared each morning to feed her, but when her stepmother found out, she dug up the vines.

Then a stream appeared, with water that was fresh and nutritious. The stepmother discovered it, and filled in the stream with earth.

In despair, the girl went back to her mother's grave. As she wept, a hunter appeared. The girl hurriedly dried her tears so that he would not see her crying.

"May I make arrows from the wood of this dead tree?" he politely asked her.

"Yes, you may," the girl replied.

The good spirit of the girl's mother was in the wood. When the hunter made his arrows, her spirit was released, causing the girl and the hunter to fall in love and get married. And the mother's spirit protected them from harm for the rest of their lives.

Moses in Pharaoh's Court

Episodes from the Bible were commonly used to explain miracles, reproach the wicked, or express a moral. In this familiar story, Pharaoh's court sorcerers are seen as hoodoo practitioners who lose their power, known as their "hand."

The Israelites were captured and carried down in bondage to Egypt. And Moses was born there. To keep the Hebrews from multiplying so fast, Pharaoh told his soldiers to kill all the little Hebrew boy babies. So when Moses was born his mother kept him hidden for three months. When she couldn't hide him any longer, she made a basket of bulrushes, and put him in it. Then she carried him down and put him in the river where Pharaoh's daughter went to bathe.

When Pharaoh's daughter found the baby, she carried him to her daddy and begged to adopt him. So he agreed, and he told her, "Go out and find you a nurse, an Israelite woman, for they'd know how to take care of this baby." And the daughter went out and hired an Israelite woman who was the baby's real mother.

The baby grew fast, and learned all the Egyptian words and languages. So Pharaoh made him a ruler then, because he saw how smart he was. One day, Moses walks out and he sees a Hebrew and an Egyptian fighting. And he kills this Egyptian, and then buries him in the sand.

A few days later, he sees two Hebrews fighting again. He said, "Why do you all strive against one another?" "Aren't you brothers?" One said, "Are you going to kill one of us like you did that Egyptian the other day?"

Moses didn't think anyone had seen what he did, and he got scared and ran away into Middin. He stayed there forty years and married an Ethiopian woman.

One day he was out minding his father-in-law's sheep, and the Lord spoke unto Moses and said, "Pull off your shoes, for you are on holy ground. I want you to go back and deliver my children from Egypt." Then the Lord said, "Moses, what is that in your hand?"

"It's a staff," said Moses.

"Cast it on the ground," said God.

The staff turned into a snake, and Moses was frightened and drew away.

The Lord said, "Go back and pick it up." So Moses picked it up, and it turned back into a staff. The Lord said, "Go back and wrought all these miracles in Egypt, and deliver my children from bondage."

So Moses goes on back. He goes in to see Pharaoh and tells him what the Lord said. Pharaoh said, "I never heard of this God. Who is he?"

"I can show you what he has the power to do," said Moses. And he cast his rod on the floor, and it turned into a serpent. Pharaoh said "That ain't nothing. My hoodoo magicians can do that." He brought in his magicians and soothsayers and they cast their rods on the floor, and theirs turned to snakes, too.

But when Pharaoh's snakes crawled up to Moses' snake, Moses' snake swallowed up their snakes. And that's where hoodoo lost his hand, because theirs was the evil power and Moses' was the good.

Hunger, Rice and Cassava

When Rice and Cassava appear in a village, the people are always happy to see them.

On the day God created people, He also created food in two forms—Rice and Cassava. Then He told them: "Remember, Cassava, the people must eat you properly cooked, otherwise you will make them sick. And you, Rice, must be boiled or eaten in soup or gravy, but never raw. Go now to the villages of the people and be their food so they may live."

Rice was ready to begin the journey, but Cassava said, "You have made my brother Rice and I the keepers of people's lives. What will happen if we are not treated with proper respect?"

God answered, "My son Hunger, who you will soon meet, has been created to teach gratitude. He will accompany you on all your journeys."

Hunger arrived. His skin was as dry as a drum-skin, and his bones were sticking out. God told him, "If the people do not show proper appreciation for their food, and do not carefully cultivate Rice and Cassava, you will make them as thin as yourself."

So the three of them set out on their journey. Whenever they approached a village, Hunger would blow in first. A terrible wind would dry the leaves and stalks, and people would become faint with their need for food.

But as soon as they could see Rice and Cassava coming down the path, the people would rush towards them, offer them water, beg them to stay forever, and thank God for sending them.

The Moon King

In this Angolan myth, a little frog plays matchmaker for the Prince of the Earth and the Moon King's daughter.

The King of the Earth had one son. When he came of age, his father told him, "You must marry. I will help you choose a wife." The prince replied, "I only want the Moon King's daughter for my wifc."

The King asked each of the wise men and women of his kingdom how to find the path to the Moon, but no one knew. Just then, the Frog spoke up. "Sire," he said, "I will travel to the Moon for you." The King did not really believe the Frog could make such a journey, but decided to give him a chance. "All right," said the King. "Take this letter to the Moon King."

The Frog knew that the Moon King's water bearers came to Earth every morning before sunrise to fetch water from a hidden spring deep in the forest. The next morning, the Frog hid in the spring, and swam into the first pail they lowered for filling.

When the water bearers returned to the Moon, the frog jumped out and asked to be taken to the Moon King. When the Frog was brought before him, he produced the Earth King's letter. The Moon King read it, wrote a reply, and handed it to the Frog who was brought back to Earth in one of the empty water pails.

He swam out when the pail was lowered into the water, hurried to the court of the Earth King, and announced himself by saying, "The Ambassador to the Moon King's court is here with a message for the Earth King."

The Earth King read the letter. The Moon King had agreed to the wedding of his daughter to the Earth prince as soon as the bride price was paid. The Earth King gave the Frog a bag of gold to take up to the Moon. When the Frog arrived, he was treated to a fine meal of pork and chicken, and then carried the message back to Earth that the Princess of the Moon would arrive the next night.

Nobody really believed the Frog, but they put on their best clothes just in case. Sure enough, the next night, the Moon Princess descended along a silver cord woven by the Moon Spider, and was married to the Prince of the Earth.

Fairy Tales

Battle Between the Birds
and the Beasts

FRANCES CARPENTER

**In this story, being big and strong is not as important
as being clever and brave.**

Birds and beasts were on this earth long before there were men and women. At least that is how one old African tale is told.

Sometimes the two, the birds and the beasts, were at peace. They lived together as brothers.

Sometimes, however, they quarreled. Then there was war between them.

It was a quarrel between an ostrich and an elephant that started the trouble this time. Oh, it was a famous battle. Many stories were told about it by the African grandmothers.

What was the quarrel about? No one knows surely. Some say the ostrich was annoyed with the elephant because that great beast did not look where he stepped as he ambled over the plain. Again and again his clumsy feet would spoil the round nest which the ostrich had dug in the earth for her eggs. It was because this happened so often that the ostrich went to the other birds. It was because she complained so bitterly that they agreed to make war on the elephant.

It was the chief of the ostrich tribe who delivered the declaration of war. With his head so high in the air, the ostrich could see far, far across the flat plain. He knew just where to go. And with his long, strong legs, he ran quickly to face his enemy.

"You have destroyed one too many of our nests, O Elephant," he shouted. "We declare war upon you. All the birds will fight with me. You, yourself, had better ask for help from the other beasts."

So the elephant called all the four-footed creatures about him. "Get ready, Friends!" he shouted. "The birds have declared war upon us."

How those animals laughed! Imagine birds, puny birds, trying to do battle with elephants! It sounded silly, indeed. But the birds did not laugh. "Wait and see who wins the battle!" they said.

It must have been a strange sight. On one side of the plain the four-footed creatures formed a long line. The monkeys were there, the leopards and lions, and of course the elephants. Great beasts and small beasts, they stood shoulder to shoulder.

On the other side of the plain were the creatures with wings. One would think that the birds would have been afraid. They were so much smaller. But size does not always mean courage, as you shall see.

"The lion and the leopard shall be my chief helpers," the elephant said. "They shall be my two generals. We three will lead the beast army in the battle."

So those three big animals took their place in the very front line.

"I choose the eagle, the falcon, and the stork to fight with me," the ostrich cried when the line of birds was drawn up.

"I myself cannot fly, for all I am a bird," the ostrich reminded his friends. "But I have made a plan of battle that will win the victory for us."

"For our weapons we shall use these eggs which my hen has laid." He pointed to three giant cream-colored balls in a round nest in the ground. With its shell, each ostrich egg would weigh several pounds.

"First the eagle shall take one egg up in his claws. He shall fly toward the animal army.

For a quick moment he shall light on the elephant's head. He shall break the egg there. Then he shall fly back again."

The birds looked at each other. They did not understand how ostrich eggs could win the battle. But they did not object, and the ostrich went on telling them of his plan.

"The falcon shall follow the eagle's example. Only, he shall break the second egg on the head of the lion. The stork will deal with the leopard."

The birds were still puzzled. But, after all, this was the ostrich's war. They would fight as he commanded.

"The eagle is coming!" The hyena, standing upon a high rock gave the warning to the beast army. But the animals were not worried. What harm could a bird do, flying up in the sky?

But before they could gather their wits together, the eagle had swooped down on the elephant. He lit on the head of the surprised beast.

Crack! Splash! The ostrich egg was broken upon the skull of the great beast. Its thick yolk was running down into the elephant's small eyes.

All the animals heard the elephant cry out.

"Oh! Oh! My head is broken open. It is bleeding and I am going to die." He had flung up his trunk to feel his head with its tip. And it had found the broken egg. The elephant, who could not see for the yolk in his eyes, thought the bits of shell were his crushed bones. The thick yolk felt like blood. And besides, the blow from the big, heavy egg had made his head ache.

"Oh! Oh! The elephant's head is broken. Oh! Oh! Our general will die." The hyena ran with this message from one end of their battle line to the other.

"And now the falcon is coming!" the hyena scout cried out a second time. "He flies toward General Lion." You remember, this was the next part of the ostrich's plan of battle.

The lion roared. But this did not stop the fierce falcon from lighting upon his head.

Crack! Splash! The falcon flung the second ostrich egg at the lion's nose.

"The lion's head is broken, too!" the hyena screamed. "Another one of our three generals will die."

The paw of the lion went round and round, trying to wipe the egg yolk out of his eyes. He, too, was blinded. He, too, was sure the wetness he felt was blood.

"Yes, my head is broken," the lion roared. "It hurts. I shall surely die." Before the beasts had time to think clearly, there came the stork, flying over the head of the leopard.

The third egg was dropped from high in the sky. It landed between the small ears of the leopard. And now all three of the generals of the animal army were in a sad state.

The beasts, without their leaders, did not know what to do. And their troubles were not over. For the ostrich had called for help from the bees. To be sure, bees are not birds. But they are creatures with wings. And they were glad to fight with their feathered friends.

By the thousands, the bees buzzed round the heads of the beasts. On their tender noses, the lion and the leopard felt their sharp stings. The bees even found tender spots in the elephant's open mouth in which they could thrust their sharp stingers. All in the army of animals felt their attack.

The generals—the elephant, the lion, and the leopard—ran away to escape the stings of the bees. Who can blame the other four-footed creatures for doing the same?

"The victory is ours!" The ostrich flapped his tiny, useless wings in joy. "The battle is over."

But there was still one beast left on the plain. This was the hyena, truly a silly creature. He had crept up behind the ostrich and he had seen the patches of pink meat that showed between the giant bird's long, thin tail feathers. How good it would be if he could have just one bite! He leaped up off the ground, but the ostrich whirled around in time.

Oh, it was terrible, the punishment which the hyena had then. The angry ostrich struck the beast with his mighty feet. And an ostrich's legs are strong enough to knock down a leopard or a lion. The poor hyena was kicked about over the plain like a leaf tossed by the wind.

All the time the furious ostrich was pecking at the hyena's head. It was just by luck that the giant bird did not find the animal's eyes.

Now the hyena is known to be a coward at heart. As soon as he could, this one ran away. He crept into a hole between some rocks where the ostrich could not get at him. He hoped that, in time, the angry bird would go away.

At last all was quiet outside the hyena's den. The animal crept to its opening, and he stuck his head out of the rocks. Quickly he drew it back again. For the ostrich was still there, walking up and down, up and down. He was still waiting for the hyena to show himself.

A little later, the hyena peeked out again. That time he only just escaped a fierce peck from the bird's beak. The same thing happened another time, and another.

The hyena would never have come out again, perhaps, if the ostrich had not grown tired of the game. Oh, that big bird was clever. Before he went off, he pulled several long feathers out of his tail. And he stuck them into the ground so that they waved across the mouth of the hole in the rock.

Two or three times the hyena peeked out. Twice he went back again, fooled by the feathers into thinking his enemy was still there. But the third time, he was so thirty and hungry, that he took a chance and slipped out of his den. And he saw how he had been tricked.

Is this story true?

Who can know?

What is sure, however, is that the hyena today makes his home in a hole in the ground, or in a den in the rocks. And he does not come out to hunt for food and drink until it is dark.

Who Can Break a Bad Habit?

FRANCES CARPENTER

> Scratching and twitching come naturally to monkeys and rabbits, and there's just nothing to be done about it.

One day, in a West African forest, a rabbit and a monkey were sitting under a tree by a river. Every few minutes the monkey scratched himself with his long finger. First he scratched his neck. Then he scratched his ribs. Stretching his long arms around him, he even scratched his back. Scratching like this is a habit of monkeys.

The rabbit, close by, was no quieter. Every few minutes he sniffed the air. His nose wrinkled and twitched. His long ears flopped as he turned his head from one side to the other. This is the way of all rabbits. They seem always afraid that some danger is near.

Each animal noticed the movements of the other. And at last the rabbit could stand the monkey's scratching no longer.

"Why do you keep scratching yourself, Friend?" he said to the monkey who was then rubbing an ear. "You are not still a minute. Always, oh, all the time your nails are digging away at your hide. This is a most annoying habit you have."

Now nobody really enjoys being scolded. And so the monkey replied in the same tone of voice.

"My habit is no more annoying than yours, my good Rabbit. You do not keep still either. Your nose wrinkles and twitches. Your long ears keep flopping. Every few minutes you turn your silly head from one side to the other as if you were afraid."

"Well, perhaps I do twitch my nose and turn my head. But I can easily stop," the rabbit declared.

"I'll bet that you can't. Although I myself could easily keep from scratching, if I really wanted to." The monkey clasped both of his forepaws together.

They argued back and forth.

"I can stop my habit, but you cannot."

"If you can, I can." So it went until at last the monkey broke off.

"We'll make a test," he suggested. "We'll see which one of us is strong enough to break his bad habit. I'll bet you I can keep quite still for the whole afternoon. And I'll bet you cannot."

"Good!" There was nothing the rabbit could do but agree. "The one who moves first will lose the bet." He gave his head one last turn, and his nose one last twitch.

There they both sat, under the tree by the West African river. Not one move did either make. But each looked very unhappy.

Never in all his life did the skin of that monkey feel so dry and itchy. The rabbit's heart was cold with his fear of the unseen danger that might be behind him. But the monkey did not scratch. The rabbit did not turn his head.

It was not really very long. A beetle passing by had crawled only a few yards along the riverbank. But it seemed to the two animals that they had not moved for a whole day.

"What shall I do?" the poor rabbit was thinking hard. "I cannot keep still very much longer. If I could only sniff once! If I could but turn my head halfway round! Then it would not be so bad."

At the same time the monkey's hide was burning and itching.

"I cannot keep from scratching much longer," the beast said to himself. "If only I could rub myself without the rabbit seeing me."

It was the rabbit who spoke first.

"The time is long, Friend Monkey. Of course I am quite comfortable. I am entirely easy in my mind, Monkey. But the sun is still high in the sky. Why should we not tell each other a story to make the afternoon pass more quickly?"

"Well, why not?" The monkey suspected the rabbit was thinking of playing some trick. But he only added, "Yes, Rabbit, let us, each one, tell a story."

"I'll begin, Monkey. I will tell you of one day last month when I was far out of this forest. I was alone in a clearing, and there was not one bush to hide me."

Here the monkey broke in. He did not yet know what trick the rabbit had thought of, but he knew he should be prepared.

"Oh, Rabbit," he cried, "that very same thing once happened to me."

"Now don't interrupt." The rabbit was impatient to get on with his tale. "I heard a noise in the tall grass on this side of me." Like any storyteller he naturally turned his head to show how it was. "I saw some hyenas running toward me. One came from this side. One came from the other side." Again and again the rabbit's head was turned to illustrate his tale.

"Other hyenas came after them. From the right; from the left; from behind; and before me." Oh, now the rabbit was having a fine time, turning his head and twitching his nose. Anyone telling of so many dangers would have to do the same thing.

The monkey soon saw what his friend was up to. The moment the rabbit stopped to get breath, he began his own story.

"One day," he cried, "I went to the village on the other side of the forest. Some boys saw me there. And they began to throw stones at me.

"One stone hit me here." The monkey reached up and rubbed his neck to show where the stone hit. Oh, it did feel good to get in just that one little scratch.

"Another stone hit me here." The monkey rubbed his shoulder. "Another! Another! And another stone came." Now the creature's paw was flying from one itching place to another.

The rabbit burst out into a laugh. He laughed and he laughed. The monkey laughed too. Each guessed the other's reason for telling his story that way.

The two animals laughed so hard that they had to hold onto each other to keep from rolling into the river.

"Well! Well!" the monkey cried. "I have not yet lost the bet."

"No more have I," said the rabbit. "We were each of us only telling a tale as it should be told."

"But we must agree, Friend," he continued, "it's very hard indeed to break a bad habit. No one ever easily changes his ways. Let us worry no more."

So the rabbit's nose wrinkled and twitched again as often as he wished. His long ears flopped as his round head turned every few minutes from one side to the other.

The monkey's paws scratched his hide wherever it itched. And from that day to this no member of either of these animal families has kept still very long unless he was asleep.

The Fairy Frog

A SWAZI TALE

TERRY BERGER

Tombi-Ende's beauty makes her sisters so jealous
that they try to get rid of her.

Tombi-Ende was the most beautiful of all the maidens in her father's kingdom. Her eyes were as brown as the eyes of the doe, and when she led the dance her feet were as quick as the feet of the gazelle. Her name, Tombi-Ende, meant "Tall Maiden," and she was indeed taller than any of her sisters. She carried her head high, like a true Princess, and her parents looked upon her with joy and pride. They expected that one day she would be a mighty Queen.

But no one has an altogether happy lot. It was true that Tombi-Ende was tall and beautiful, and that she had the gayest and most wonderful handkerchiefs with which to deck herself, and more beads and bracelets than any other girl in the countryside. But she also had sisters who were not so tall or beautiful or so greatly admired, and who grew more jealous of her daily. At last, this jealousy grew so intense that it made them quite forget their love for her, and they decided that Tombi-Ende must disappear or no one would ever notice them at all.

And so the jealous sisters worked out a plan to rid themselves of Tombi-Ende. One day they went to her and said, "Come with us. Let us go to the great pit to dig up red ochre, for there is none to be had in the kraal." So every maiden shouldered her pick, and they all walked together, singing and laughing, for many miles. At last they reached a great red pit, many feet deep, surrounded by tall grass on every side. There they stopped; and each girl leaped down in turn to dig out a lump of the precious red earth, and then jumped up again. But when it came time for Tombi-Ende to jump down, the others did not let her jump up again. Instead, each of the jealous sisters threw picks full of earth upon her, until the poor maiden was buried alive. This done, they ran back to their village leaving their sister behind.

When they arrived home, they told their father that Tombi-Ende had accidentally fallen into the pit and before they could help her to escape, she had suffocated before their eyes. But unfortunately for the girls, each sister told the story in a different way, and the King doubted their innocence in the matter. Ordering his servants to lock all of them into a hut, the King began to mourn for his favorite daughter, for Tombi-Ende the Tall Maiden.

Surprisingly enough, Tombi-Ende was not dead. Although the red earth was very heavy, she was able to breathe through the breaks in the great mound of red ochre that lay above her. And she began to cry out:

I am Tombi-Ende,
I am not dead,
I am alive like one of you.

For many hours she lay in the red ochre pit, chanting the same call, though fearing more and more that she would never be rescued. When evening came, however, she thought she heard a croaking sound. And indeed she did for at the edge of the pit stood an enormous frog.

"Beautiful Princess," he croaked, "what has befallen you?"

Hearing this question, the lovely maiden cried out in reply, "Alas! My sisters are jealous of me and hate me, and they have thrown earth upon me and left me here, hoping that I would never get out."

"Do not grieve," said the frog, "I will help you." And with that, he jumped into the pit, tunneled through the earth to the Princess, opened his big mouth, and swallowed the Princess in one gulp. Then he jumped up out of the pit, landing directly on the path above, with the Princess safely inside of him.

From there the frog set out upon a long journey. He hopped all night, taking care to avoid any kraals along the way, for the people believed frogs to be an omen of bad luck and he would not have been welcomed. Whenever he passed a bird he sang out:

> Do not swallow me,
> I carry the Princess Tombi-Ende.

And no creature touched him. Though the next morning they vary narrowly escaped a great danger, for they came upon a horrible ogress. This Imbula had heard that Tombi-Ende was still alive and had gone in search of her, but when she arrived at the red ocher pit, she had found it empty. Now she was looking for the Princess everywhere, dashing about in a frenzied state, but luckily she paid no attention to the big frog.

At midday the frog stopped hopping. He opened his large mouth, allowing the Princess to step out.

"Wait here and rest," said the frog, "and then we will go on." He croaked three times, and delicious porridge appeared in a little brown pot, all ready for the Princess to eat.

Tombi-Ende ate and soon fell asleep under the bushes, for she was very tired. When evening came, the frog swallowed her once more and they continued on their journey. They had decided not to go to her father's kraal, for fear of her jealous sisters, but rather to go to the home of her grandmother, where Tombi-Ende was sure of every welcome. The frog hopped all through the night, and when morning came he arrived at the grandmother's kraal. Hopping up to the chief hut, the frog sang out loudly:

> I am carrying Tombi-Ende,
> The beautiful Princess
> Whom they buried in the red pit.

Out came the old grandmother, crying out, "Who is speaking? Who knows what has become of my darling Tombi-Ende?"

"It is I that knows all about her," replied the frog. "Bring clean mats to spread before me, and you will see." All the women hurried to get fine new mats, and these they placed before the frog. When this was done, the frog croaked loudly; and opening his mouth as large as before, he allowed the Princess to come out. The women almost fainted as they saw Tombi-Ende standing before them, as tall and beautiful as ever. But their surprise soon turned to joy and there was not one among them who could hear the Princess tell her tale often enough, or sing often enough the praises of the wonderful frog.

"What can we do to reward your kindness?" the grandmother asked of the frog. "There must be something that we can give you."

The frog thought for a moment. "I will only ask you to kill two oxen and two bulls," he said, "and to lay a feast before me."

So a great feast was held, and the frog sat by the Princess's side and was given great honor. He seemed very pleased by the many preparations that had been made on his behalf. The next morning, however, the frog had disappeared, and although the Princess searched for him throughout the kraal, he could not be found.

In the meantime, the grandmother had sent a messenger to the King, telling him of his daughter's safety. Upon hearing that all was well, the King was beside himself with joy. First, he released the jealous sisters from their prison, instructing them to prepare robes of state for Tombi-Ende. Then he dispatched his favorite son to bring the Princess home.

The boy arrived, rested a few days at the grandmother's kraal, and then the two set out for home. Great heat and dry earth were their companions on the journey, for the rains had been meager that year and the streams had dried up. The sun was very hot and after hours of walking, the Princess and her brother became very thirsty. Even the underground springs could not be found, for the earth was harder than brick that is dried in an oven, and the water courses were dry. After a time they began to feel faint from the intense heat.

Suddenly, as if in a dream, they saw a strange man standing right across their path. Except for his large size, he appeared to be like other men, and they greeted him with thanksgiving.

"What do you want?" he asked them in a voice that surprised them, for it was of the deepest bass and it rumbled like thunder.

"We are looking for water," said the Prince. "We find that all of the springs are dried up, and we are still many days from home."

"If I should give you water," bargained the giant, "what will you give me in return?"

"You may ask for anything in my father's kingdom," the Prince answered without thinking.

"I will take this beautiful Princess," said the giant, with a wicked smile playing on his lips. "If you do not give me what I ask for, you will die of thirst. All of the springs are dry within the next three day's journey."

The trials of the past were nothing to the grief and unhappiness that Tombi-Ende and her brother now suffered. What were they to do? To grant the stranger's request might prove fatal for the Princess, but a further lack of water would leave them both helpless. The only solution was to accept the giant's offer and to pray that he would treat them with mercy.

When they agreed to the giant's terms, he chuckled for a few minutes and then led the way to a great fig tree by the side of a dry water course. As he struck his stick upon the ground, a fountain sprang from the very roots of the tree, and its water was as clear as the moon and as cool as the depths of the forest. The brother and sister plunged themselves into the water, allowing it to bathe their faces while they drank of it eagerly and long.

After some time, Tombi-Ende lifted her head, and as her eyes met with the giant, she let out a shriek, for the giant had turned into a most horrible Inzimu. He was monstrous and misshapen, covered with red hair. Behind him on the grass, lay his long tail, and his white pointed teeth forced his thick lips to remain open.

Frightened by his sister's screams, the Prince looked up. Seeing the monstrous Inzimu, he realized at once just how dangerous their situation was. The ogre was very powerful, and no fighting could possibly save them. He just kept glaring at them, through tiny eyes that radiated evil pleasure.

For Tombi-Ende and her brother, the end seemed to have come; but suddenly there was a loud croak, and out of the fountain sprang the giant frog.

"Save me!" cried Tombi-Ende. "Oh help us, frog! No one is as clever and as wise as you!"

The large frog hopped right up to the ogre. The ogre looked down at the frog with disdain and laughed at him with disbelief. The frog allowed the ogre to laugh in this way for a few minutes and then, opening his mouth as large as he could, he swallowed the ogre up, tail and all. At once the frog jumped back into the fountain, and there he remained until the ogre was drowned. Then he returned to Tombi-Ende.

"Ah, my frog, how can I thank you enough?" asked the Princess. "This time you must not disappear. You must come home with us, to be honored as is your due."

And so in three days, Tombi-Ende, her brother, and the frog reached the kraal of the King. As they arrived, they were greeted by the King's guard; beautifully arrayed in otter skins and holding shields and assegais. At their head stood the King, who hailed his two children with joy and affection.

"But why," he inquired, "is that horrible frog at your side? I cannot bear to look at him; let us have him killed."

"Oh, no, father," gasped Tombi-Ende, "do not kill him, for he is the best of creatures; twice he saved my life. If it were not for this frog, you would see your Tombi-Ende no more."

As she spoke these words, the frog suddenly turned into the handsomest of men, taller even than Tombi-Ende herself. He was dressed in a splendid array of skins and white ostrich plumes, and everyone could see that he was a Prince. Loud, happy shouts greeted him; but the Princess, herself, did not seem too surprised to see what had happened.

"I am no frog," said the Prince. "My father is a great Chief. The ogre, from whom I rescued the Princess, bewitched me in days gone by. But now that I have won the heart of a maiden, I am free once more. Please, sir, give me the hand of your beloved daughter in marriage, and one hundred cattle shall be yours."

And so a few days later, Tombi-Ende married the fairy frog, an end to the story that brought joy to them both. As for the wicked sisters, the King forgave them, and Tombi-Ende soon forgot all they had done and thought only of her happiness in her new home.

The Magic Bones

Two brothers could have lived happily-ever-after if they had not been so jealous and greedy.

There once were three brothers who were left orphans during a great famine. When the youngest of them became ill, the two elder brothers did not know what to do. Then one proposed, "Let us take him into the veld and nurse him. Maybe he will recover there." So they carried him far into the bush.

After some time the two elders again wondered what to do with their youngest brother as he was not getting better. "It is a time of famine," said one to the other. "We have no food. Let us leave him here and return home."

When the sick one heard this he pleaded, "Please do not leave me here alone." But they left him, and went on their way.

Eventually, the youngest brother recovered, and began to set snares to catch game. One day he set his snares on the site of an old village. The next morning, when he went to check them, he found an old man caught in one of them. He stood some distance away, afraid to go nearer, but the old man called out, "Come nearer, boy, come here to me!"

When the boy approached, the old man asked, "Who told you to set snares here?"

"No one," said the boy, "but I was hungry. How was I to eat?"

"Put your hand into my bag," said the old man, "and draw out my magic bones."

The boy did as he was bid.

"Do you want some porridge?" asked the old man.

"Yes," the boy quickly answered, "for I am very hungry."

"Throw the bones and say, 'Let porridge come forth at once.'"

The boy did so, and behold, porridge came forth.

As the boy ate, the old man said, "I shall soon die. My name is Jirimpimbira (which means "jumping shin-bone"). Don't forget that name when I am dead, for I am leaving it to you. When you wander about you will reach a wide plain. Throw the bones and you will get a dwelling and all you desire." With that the old man died.

The boy wandered about and at last came to a wide plain. He threw the bones, saying, "Let there be a large village and lots of food." Instantly, a large village, full of people, appeared. Many came out shouting "Jirimpimbira!" begging for food for there was another great famine.

Now the two brothers who had left their brother in the bush heard from others that there was a chief named Jirimpimbira who had plenty of food, so they decided to go to him in the hopes of obtaining something to eat.

The chief saw them coming, clapping their hands in salutation, and shouting "Jirimpimbira!" He gave each a bowl of milk and asked them to drink, then said, "Have you forgotten me? I am your youngest brother, the one you left in the bush."

When they heard this they wept. "We left our brother in the veld when hunger overcame us. Please forgive us!" Then the chief gave wives to each and said, "My brothers, stay here and live with me. Look upon this place as yours."

At first the brothers were very happy, but after several months, they became envious, and said to each other, "Why should our younger brother be chief? We are the elders." They went to their brother's wife to find out the secret of how he had obtained so large a village. They flattered her until she told them the secret. While Jirimpimbira was away cultivating his fields, the brothers begged her to show them the bones.

"If I let you see them, what will you give me?" she asked.

"Whatever you desire," they said.

"If you bring me the flesh of a hare, I will show you the bones," she replied.

They readily agreed and immediately went away to hunt. Soon they returned with two fat hares for the woman.

She gave them the bones, telling them that when they reached a place they liked, they were to throw the bones and a village would appear.

The brothers ran away with the bones. When they came to a suitable spot, they threw the bones on the ground and asked for a large village with much food. Instantly, it appeared. Then they threw the bones a second time, saying, "Let Jirimpimbira's village disappear." Immediately it vanished, and Jirimpimbira found himself all alone.

Jirimpimbira lamented, "My brothers have got hold of my magic bones! Again they have left me all alone!" Just then, Gonzo, the rat, appeared. "Why do you cry, Jirimpimbira?" he asked.

"I cry for the loss of my bones which I know my brothers have stolen."

Then Ngabi, the hawk, who happened to float over him, asked, "Why do you cry, Jirimpimbira?"

"I cry for the loss of my bones which I know my brothers have stolen."

Then Gonzo and Ngabi said, "Do not cry. We will get the bones and bring them back to you."

Jirimpimbira rejoiced at this, and told them he would be most grateful for their help.

"What will you give us if we return the bones to you?" they asked.

"Anything you desire," he replied.

"I want chickens," Ngabi answered. "And I want nuts," said Gonzo.

The rat ran along while the hawk flew high in the air. When Ngabi reached the village of the two brothers he hovered in the air, waiting for Gonzo to arrive.

Gonzo was sure the bones were being kept in the largest house. He crept in and scurried up the wall. He nibbled through the string by which the bones were tied, and then carried them outside. Once outside, people began to shout, "The Chief's magic bones are being carried away by a rat!" But just then Ngabi swooped down, picked up Gonzo with the magic bones, and flew away. When the people saw this, they cried out, "Toko! (Well done!) The rat is being carried off by the hawk." Of course, they thought the hawk would eat the rat.

The hawk carried Gonzo and the magic bones to Jirimpimbira who thanked them for what they had done. He then threw the bones and said, "Let there be nuts and chickens for Gonzo and Ngabi."

Then he threw the bones again, saying, "I want my village and all I had returned to me." His village and its people appeared. He threw the bones again, saying, "May the village of my brothers be scattered and no trace of it remain." And no one ever heard of or saw the two brothers ever again.

Timba, the Dissatisfied Bird

Timba gets everything he asks for, but it still isn't enough.

Strangely enough, two very different creatures of the wilds—Ngango, the mighty lion, and Timba, the little brown robin—had formed a friendship.

It began when Timba noticed that from time to time, the lion made kills that were too large for him to finish at one meal. This meant that part of the carcass was left to rot—and rotting meat meant big, juicy white maggots, which were Timba's favorite food.

It was, therefore, easy to understand why Timba took to following Ngango from one hunting ground to another, listening for his roar of victory each time he made a kill. "*This is my hunting-ground; this is my hunting-ground!*" the lord of the forest would roar, as he stood majestically on the top of the highest ant-heap to let all the creatures know that they were to bow down to him. Of course, no one dreamed of opposing him—especially the little brown robin.

The lion had no objection to Timba benefiting from his leavings. Day after day the big cat would chat amiably with the little bird who sat twittering in excited anticipation in the tree above him, waiting for the maggots to ripen.

"*Tii-tii-tii-tii-tii!*" trilled the robin, his song making the countryside glad with music. "Great is the strength of Ngango. Wise is the rule of his law!" Then one day he added, "But oh, *why* am I so small and insignificant?"

Ngango always enjoyed listening to Timba's flattering song, and he was in a particularly good mood that morning. "Yes, my friend," Ngango said, "all you sing of me is true, and it is indeed unfortunate that you are of so little account. If you were of greater importance, your song would carry more weight among my subjects. But why do you shame yourself by eating my rotten leavings, instead of hunting good, red meat of your own?"

"Indeed, wise Ngango, I agree with all that you say," answered the little bird sadly, "but I am too small to catch anything else. Oh, that I were bigger and stronger and fiercer!"

"I can help you to become so, should you wish," said the lion pleasantly.

"Oh, Lord of the Forest, Mighty One, please do so!" trilled the little robin.

"Then we must visit Fisi, the witch-doctor," said the lion. "Come, I will take you to him."

They found Fisi the hyena lying asleep at the entrance to his bone-littered cave. The lion's loud greeting sent the ugly creature scuttling into the shadows behind him. "Fisi, my brave fellow," laughed the lion, "I have some work for you to do. Our friend Timba is tired of being so small and insignificant that he is forced to eat the worms that live in the leavings of other people's kills. He wishes to be changed into a fierce animal who can catch and kill meat for himself. Please mix a suitable potion for him."

The hyena went back into the gloom of his cluttered cave. He soon returned with the desired mixture which he gave to the robin. No sooner had the little bird swallowed it, than he changed into Lilongwe, a fierce little gray mongoose. He was delighted, and immediately went into the forest to hunt rats, birds, and other small creatures.

Things went well to begin with, but after a while the lion and mongoose met. "Well, Lilongwe, how are you getting on?" asked the lion.

"Not so well as I could wish," grumbled the mongoose. "Birds are difficult to catch. Besides, it is the good, red blood of *animal* flesh that I crave. If only Fisi had mixed a little stronger potion for me," he added wistfully.

"Very well," said the lion with an indulgent smile, "we will visit him again and see if he will help you further."

They repeated their visit to the witch-doctor's cave, and Fisi mixed another magic brew at the lion's request. No sooner had the mongoose swallowed it, than in his place stood a sleek and velvety spotted leopard. Nyalugwe, we now must call him, purred with pride and pleasure, and at once bounded into the forest to hunt small buck, hares, and baboons.

For some time the leopard was contented with his lot, but eventually he thought how very much more exciting it would be to hunt in the open by daylight, instead of keeping to the shadows of the dark forest. Besides, he wanted to kill big animals—zebra and buffalo—not little things like baboons and rock rabbits. The more he thought about it, the more dissatisfied he became with his present lot.

It was not long after this that Ngango saw Nyalugwe slinking along a path in the depth of the forest one morning just after sunrise. "Good morning, my friend," the lion greeted him, "I am sure you must be quite satisfied now."

"Not completely," replied the leopard irritably. "I wish I could catch big animals like you do."

"Very well," said the lion patiently, "we will visit Fisi once more." So they went to the witch-doctor's cave for the third time. When the hyena had prepared an extra large potion, the lion took it and, before handing it to Nyalugwe he said, "I must make one condition before your next change takes place. When you have made your kills, you are never, never, ever to roar like I do because, as you are well aware, all the hunting in this area belongs to me. In my roar I am entitled to say '*This is my hunting-ground; this is my hunting-ground.*' You must say, '*This is Ngango's hunting-ground; this is Ngango's hunting-ground!*' If you disobey this order, you will be punished. Do you understand?"

The leopard thumped the ground sulkily upon each side of him, with his elegant, yellow and black tail. After he had promised to follow the lion's instructions, Ngango handed the leopard the magic potion. Nyalugwe could hardly wait to gulp it down, and as soon as he did, a fine young lion appeared—strong and well-built, but smaller than Ngango. Soundlessly the young lion slipped into the tall grass at the edge of the forest, and at once began to stalk and hunt big game upon the plains.

His first kill was a buck, and the following day he killed a young kudu. This was life, indeed! How proud he felt as he dragged the various carcasses to the top of an ant-hill, as he had seen Ngango do, and from there to announce to all, "*This is Ngango's hunting-ground; this is Ngango's hunting-ground!*" before settling down to his meal. The big lion heard him, and was pleased.

The young lion went from one success to another, his kills becoming larger and larger, until finally he pulled down a big buffalo. "Surely," he said to himself with pride, as he dragged the body of the big beast to the highest point that he could find, "I am now a match for any creature living. I have as much right to this hunting-ground as any other lion." And he roared, for all to hear, "*This is MY hunting-ground; this is MY hunting-ground!*"

The king of the wilds heard the boastful roar, and hastened to where the young lion was tearing chunks of meat from his kill. "What did I hear you roar?" the older lion asked in an icy tone, as he bared his huge yellow teeth.

The young lion's heart skipped a beat or two. Perhaps, he thought, it had been unwise of him to declare his strength *quite* so soon. Maybe he should have waited until he had reached full maturity, and was certain that he could overcome the mighty Ngango. "I spoke without thinking," he said hesitantly.

"That is no excuse," growled Ngango. "Tell me," he continued in a more pleasant tone, "what were you before Fisi changed you into a lion?"

"I was a leopard," mumbled the ungrateful one. What happened then, happened so quickly that the young lion was not aware of the change until it had taken place. Looking down at his paws, he saw the earlier spotted fur of the leopard to which he had returned!

His head reeled, but he was brought back to his senses by the older lion asking him, "And before you were a leopard?"

"I was a mongoose," muttered the leopard, now very unsure of himself. He was startled to see how enormous Ngango had suddenly become, until he realized that it was he, himself, who had grown small again, for he was once more Lilongwe, a fierce little gray mongoose.

But the lion had not finished with him yet. "Yes," went on the Lord of the Wilds, "of course, a mongoose. I remember. And before that?"

"I was a robin," stammered the mongoose. The words had barely left his mouth, before he was once more Timba, the tiny little insignificant brown bird of the beginning of this tale. "*Tii-tii-tii,*" he chirped, as he fluttered up into the tree above the lion, to begin once more, his permanent search for big, juicy white maggots.

Therefore, it is always wise to show gratitude for the good things that are given to you in life, for the Great One Who gives them, can also take them away from those who do not appreciate His gifts.

Folk Tales

had not, we would all now be living in the Garden of Eden and I would never go hungry. That is why I say it is the fault of Adam."

"I see," said the king. "You work hard yet you go hungry. It does not seem fair that you are suffering because of Adam's mistake. I will help you."

The king called his chief adviser. "Have Iyapo washed and dressed. Bring him to the palace and let him stay in one of the rooms there. Take his rags and wood away. He will have a new life."

Then he said to Iyapo, "From now on you can call me brother. We will share everything. You can do anything you like except for one thing—you may not open the green door at the end of the hall. That is the one thing you may never do. Do you understand?"

"Oh, my king," cried the happy Iyapo, "what reason do I have to open the green door? I have food, clothes, and shelter. What more could I want?"

And so the woodcutter began a life of comfort. He never had to get up early or work hard. He had so much to eat he was even starting to get fat.

He had forgotten all about the green door until one day he happened to pass by it, and as he did he remembered it was the door he was never to open. However, he couldn't help wondering why he, the king's brother, was not allowed to find out what was in the room behind the door. He sighed and walked on.

During the next few days, Iyapo seemed to be drawn to the green door. Several times a day he found himself outside the door, and each time he was getting more and more curious as to what was behind it. Sometimes, without realizing it, his hand actually moved towards the handle but he managed to stop himself each time.

One day, the king said, "Brother, I have been called away to another town, and I will not be back until late today. I am entrusting the palace to you. Please take care that nothing happens."

After the king left, the woodcutter started thinking, "I am responsible for the palace so surely I also am responsible for the room behind the green door as well. I must be for I am the king's brother and have been left in charge. I am going to find out what is hidden there."

After checking that no one was looking, he put his ear against the door. He could not hear anything.

"I must know what is in there. I will just open the door a crack and close it again. The king will never know." And so he opened the door slightly. The room was dark, but after a while he could see that all that was in there were the old rags he used to wear and the wood he used to sell. Just then, a mouse ran out the door.

"Oh, no!" cried Iyapo. "The king was hiding a mouse in the room and now it has escaped. I must catch it." As he ran after the mouse, his shoes fell off. He tripped over the bottom of his long fancy robes, and had to take them off. Still, he could not catch the mouse, and he was now very hot and out of breath. Suddenly, the king appeared. He had returned early!

"What are you doing, Iyapo?" boomed the king. "Why are you running around the palace without your clothes?"

Poor Iyapo threw himself at the king's feet. "I'm sorry," he sobbed. "I did not mean to let your mouse go."

"What mouse?" asked the king. "I have no mouse."

"The mouse in the room. When I opened the green door . . ."

"You opened the green door?"

"I did not mean to. It was wrong, but my feet kept taking me there and I was curious and . . ."

"Iyapo, I am very disappointed in you. Opening the green door was the one thing I told you not to do."

"I know, sire, but I am the brother of the king and . . ."

"And now you want to be the king himself," shouted the king. "You are worse than Adam. You should have learned from his mistake."

"I am sorry, my lord. It will never happen again. I promise. What do you wish me to do?"

The king's anger had disappeared. Now he had tears in his eyes. "Go back to the room," he said sadly, "and take your rags and sticks. Return to the market and sell your wood."

"Yes, sire," was all the woodcutter could say.

"And remember this—others cannot make you happy. It is up to you and your fate. Go and work hard and know that your poverty is not the fault of Adam or anyone else."

And so Iyapo returned to the market. Once again he shouted, "Wood for sale. Who wants to buy good wood?" But he never mentioned Adam again.

Dividing the Cheese

When the monkey cheats the cats out of their cheese, they've gotten just what they deserve.

Two cats stole a cheese. Neither thought the other would divide it equally so they agreed to ask the monkey to do it.

"With pleasure," said the monkey. He sent the cats to fetch a scale. Then he got out his knife. But instead of cutting the cheese in half, he made one portion larger than the other. He put both pieces on the scale. "I didn't divide this quite right," he said. "I'll just even it up."

The monkey began to eat the cheese from the heavier side. As he ate, the heavier side became lighter than the other piece. Then he changed over and began to eat from the other side.

The cats, watching their snack disappear, said, "We've changed our mind. Please, let us have the rest of the cheese, and we will divide it ourselves."

"No, a fight might arise between you, and then the king of animals would be angry with me," said the monkey.

And he continued to eat, first on one side, and then on the other, until all the cheese was gone.

Kimwaki and the Weaver Birds

A young man squanders his inheritance until he learns that it is more satisfying to give than receive.

As an old man lay dying, he sent for his only child, a young man named Kimwaki. "My son," the father said, "I have lived a long life, and the time has come for me to join my ancestors. My years have not been spent idly. I leave you the fairest fields in the village, and the largest herd of cows and goats. Now carry me beneath the stars, for I am ready to die."

After the burial ceremony, Kimwaki looked around him and counted his wealth. It was, he realized, great for such a young man. "I have no need to ever toil again," he thought.

Day after day Kimwaki lay dreaming in the sunshine. When the sun became too hot for comfort, he lay in the shade of a big tree that grew beside his hut. He let his lovely garden become overgrown by weeds and grass. His sleek and glossy cattle, with no one to drive them to their pastures, became hollow-eyed and thin. The little goats bleated in distress.

But Kimwaki did not care, because his wise and thrifty father had also left him overflowing food bins. He felt he would always have enough. Hunger would never touch him.

In a land where it is the custom for each neighbor to help the other, not a soul lifted a finger to assist this lazy youth who gave no help to others. Though things for Kimwaki went from bad to worse, no one cared. Kimwaki was shunned by all around him.

Kimwaki led this useless life for many months, until he began to tire of the loneliness.

Then one day in early spring, while Kimwaki was napping as usual beneath his tree, he was awakened by excited twittering and singing. Annoyed, he opened his eyes to see what had disturbed his pleasant sleep. Up in the tree was a flock of little weaver birds, darting here and there. They were all as busy as could be, for it was nesting time.

Spring was in the air, and the male weaver birds were building nests in which to raise their young. Their excited twittering and busy activity made Kimwaki open his eyes a little wider to watch the birds as they worked together. Before long, the lazy boy could not help noticing what joy the birds found in working together.

Chattering and singing, each male bird did his share to build the colony. One would bring a tiny piece of grass, another a little twig, while yet another added a feather to his nest. Busily the birds worked, as though their very lives depended upon the timely completion of their task—which, indeed, it did. When evening came, the frames of the little nests were completed.

On the following day the same activities took place. The clever birds used their tiny beaks to weave the grasses in and out, lining the nest with the softest down.

Kimwaki watched it all from beneath the big tree. By the time the second evening came, thunderclouds were gathering in the sky. Kimwaki thought how wise the little weaver birds were to provide shelter for their babies against the coming rains.

Every day Kimwaki watched the diligent feathered workers. In a short while, a whole colony of finished nests hung from the branches of the tree. And during all this time, the lesson of the birds' cooperation and their hard work had been making quite an impression on Kimwaki.

Finally, the young man said to himself, "I am a strong young man, while they are only tiny birds. I have two big hands with which to work, while each of them has only a little beak. They are safe and sheltered, and I am not. Surely the birds are wiser than I am!"

He thought the matter over that night, and the next morning he rose early. Taking his rusty hoe with him, he went to the field that belonged to his nearest neighbor. There

Kimwaki began to dig and clear the weeds and grass away. When this was done, he started to hoe the ground.

All day long Kimwaki worked in a friendly way with others who joined him. When evening came, he found himself singing as he returned to his dilapidated hut. He felt as happy and lighthearted as the little weaver birds!

Day after day Kimwaki went unbidden, first to the garden of one neighbor and then to another, helping where he could and asking nothing in return.

Then one morning he awoke to hear cheerful chattering and laughter coming from his own overgrown garden.

He looked out and saw all his neighbors as busy as could be, clearing and hoeing his weed-covered fields. He joined them at once, and soon the plot of ground was ready for planting.

Later, when the rains came, his neighbors helped him plant his crops and repair his leaking hut.

The season progressed, and Kimwaki's crop grew. As the maize, beans, and potatoes grew, so grew his pride in achievement. The young man no longer wasted his days beneath the big tree, but continued to help those around him. He also saw to the comfort of his neglected flocks. He watched happily as the glow of health returned to the once-dull coats of his cows and goats.

Before long, Kimwaki's crops were ready to be harvested. His willing neighbors helped him in the fields, thereby returning the help that Kimwaki had so generously given them. And when all the grain had been winnowed and stored away, and his potatoes and beans sold at the market, Kimwaki found to his joy that once more his father's fields had yielded the highest return in the land.

Kimwaki gave thanks to the little weaver birds for showing him that only through hard work and sharing can peace, security, and happiness be found.

Rooster in a Huff

Rooster's rude behavior costs him a delicious dinner
and a very good time.

All the animals—the ducks, hens, turkeys, geese, pigs—were invited to a big supper and dance at the next farmyard. They were all looking forward to the party, and when it was time to go, they lined up to walk over. The big farmyard rooster led the way, strutting and crowing as he marched. Never have you heard such merry-making noise with all that quacking, clucking, gobbling, and oinking.

After some square dancing to sharpen their appetites, they were invited into the supper room. In the center was a huge table filled with plates piled high with food. But when they got closer, all the plates seemed to be heaped with nothing but cornbread.

Well, now, the rooster got upset when he saw this. "I can get all the cornbread I want at home," he sniffed. So he went off in a huff. But the others were having too good a time to care about what was being served, and besides, they were hungry and ready to eat anything. No sooner had they eaten the outside of the cornbread than they discovered that underneath was a huge pile of bacon and greens. And at the bottom of that were pies and cakes and other good things.

Rooster was upset when he realized what he had walked away from. But word of what he had said was out, and no one ever knew Rooster to admit he was wrong.

Now, whenever Rooster sees some food in front of him, he always scratches around the place with his feet, and he never stops scratching until he gets to the bottom of it.

How Tortoise Grew a Tail

In this Yoruba tale, the tortoise chooses just the right example to teach his friend the boa a lesson.

Ijapa the tortoise had been on a long journey under the hot sun. After walking for many hours he was tired, hot, and hungry. At this point, he was outside the house of his friend, Ojola, the boa. He went to the door and called to him, certain he would get something to eat. Ojola, seeing that Ijapa was hot and tired, invited him in.

"Come in, Ijapa, and rest awhile. You are hot and tired. Please sit down and make yourself comfortable."

So Ijapa came in and they sat down together to talk. Meanwhile, Ojola's wife was cooking, and the tortoise could smell the wonderful aroma coming from the pot. He began to groan with hunger.

"Does the smell of the cooking bother you?" asked the boa.

"No, it just reminds me of home, where I would be eating a lovely supper cooked by my wife," replied Ijapa.

"Well, tonight you will eat with us," said Ojola. "You go and wash and all will be ready."

So Ijapa went out back to wash in the stream. Feeling refreshed, he came back inside to find that a large bowl of hot steaming vegetable sand corn was already set down in the middle of the floor.

"Mmm!" said Ijapa, licking his lips. "That smells good."

"Just come here and help yourself," said Ojola wrapping himself around the bowl, and eagerly beginning to eat.

The tortoise, seeing the boa's thick coils wrapped around the bowl, walked to the other side to find a way in. But on all sides Ojola's fat coils were piled up around the bowl while he slurped and supped.

For a moment, Ojola raised his head. "This is delicious, Ijapa," he said. "What are you waiting for? Do join me before it's all gone."

"Yes, I would like to join you, Ojola, but why do you wrap yourself around the food? I can't get near it."

"This is our custom," said the boa. "We always eat our food like this. Do come quickly and have some."

Poor Ijapa scuttled this way and that and couldn't find a way in. Finally, the boa swallowed the last mouthful.

"Well, it is so nice to eat with friends," said Ojola. "We must do this again."

The tortoise did not complain, but he left Ojola's house in a bad mood—and hungrier than ever. When he got home he thought about how he could teach the boa a lesson. He decided to invite him over to his own house for the next festival day to return his hospitality.

While Ijapa's wife prepared a special festival meal, he busied himself weaving a long fat tail out of grass. When it was finished he stuck it on himself with tree-gum.

When Ojola arrived the tortoise greeted him at the door and invited him in.

"Come on, Ojola, and make yourself comfortable."

So the boa came in and they sat down together to talk. Ojola could smell the wonderful aroma coming from the cooking pot and began to lick his lips.

"That cooking smells good, Ijapa. When are we going to eat?"

"Let's eat right away," said the tortoise. "you go and wash and all will be ready."

So Ojola went out to the spring to wash. Feeling refreshed, he came back inside to find that a big feast was laid out in the middle of the floor.

"Mmm!" said Ojola, licking his lips. "That smells good."

"Just come here and help yourself," said Ijapa as he circled round and round the food until his fat tail surrounded it on all sides. Then the tortoise began to eat.

Ojola, seeing the tortoise's strange new tail wrapped around the food, slithered around to the other side to find a way in. But Ijapa's tail was piled up around the food while he slurped and supped.

"This is delicious," said Ijapa. "What are you waiting for, Ojola? Do join me before it's all gone."

"Yes, I would like to join you, Ijapa, but where did you get this big new tail? Before you were short, but now you're very long, and your tail is in my way."

"One learns about such things from one's friends," replied the tortoise.

Then Ojola remembered how when Ijapa was his guest he had wrapped his tail around the food and prevented the tortoise from eating. Ojola was ashamed. Without saying another word he went home.

From that occurrence comes the proverb:

We learn from our friends to be short
And we also learn to be tall.

Wiley and the Hairy Man

After tricking the Hairy Man three times, brave little Wiley and his momma know they won't be bothered anymore.

Before Wiley headed off into the swamp, his momma called to him. "Wiley," she said, "the Hairy Man's done got your papa, so when you're in the swamp, watch out that he don't get you."

"Yes'm," he said. "I'll look out. I'll take my hound dogs everywhere I go. The Hairy Man can't stand no hound dog."

Wiley knew that because his momma had told him, and she knew because she knew conjure.

So Wiley took his ax and went down to the swamp to cut some poles for a hen roost and his hounds went with him. But they took off after a wild pig and chased it so far that Wiley couldn't even hear them yelp.

"Well," he said, "I hope the Hairy Man ain't anywhere around here now."

He picked up his ax to start cutting the poles but before he could take the first swing, there came the Hairy Man with a big grin on his ugly face. He was hairy all over, his eyes burned like fire, and spit drooled all over his big teeth.

Wiley threw down his ax and climbed up a big bay tree. He noticed that the Hairy Man had feet like a cow, and so was pretty sure the Hairy Man couldn't climb a tree.

"Why'd you climb up there?" the Hairy Man asked Wiley from the bottom of the tree.

Wiley looked down from the very top of the tree. "My momma told me to stay away from you. What you got in that big croaker-sack?"

"Nothing," said the Hairy Man.

"Go on, get away from here," said Wiley.

The Hairy Man picked up Wiley's ax and started swinging. Chips were flying from the trunk of the big bay tree. Wiley grabbed the tree close, rubbed his belly against it and hollered, "Fly, chips, fly back in your same place."

The chips flew back in place, making the Hairy Man stomp and fume. Then he picked up the ax and started swinging faster than before. They both went to it—Wiley hollering and the Hairy Man chopping. Wiley hollered till he was hoarse, and he saw the Hairy Man was gaining on him.

"I'll come down part way," said Wiley, "if you'll make this bay tree twice as big around."

"I ain't studyin' you," said the Hairy Man, still swinging the ax.

"I bet you can't."

"I ain't gonna try."

Then they went to it again—Wiley hollering and the Hairy Man chopping. Wiley had about yelled himself out when he heard his hound dogs yelping way off.

"Hyeaaah, dog, Hyeaaah," he hollered.

"You ain't got no dogs. I sent that pig to draw them off."

"Hyeaaah, dog. Hyeaaah," hollered Wiley, and they both heard the hound dogs yelping and coming closer. The Hairy Man looked worried.

"Come on down and I'll teach you conjure," he said.

"I can learn all the conjure I want from my momma," said Wiley.

The Hairy Man grit his teeth. He threw the ax down and took off through the swamp.

When Wiley got home he told his momma that the Hairy Man had almost got him, but that the dogs ran him off.

"Did he have his sack?"

"Yes'm."

"Next time he comes after you, don't climb any trees. Just stay on the ground and say, 'Hello, Hairy Man.' Okay, Wiley?"

"No'm."

"He ain't gonna hurt you, child. Just do like I say. You say, 'Hello, Hairy Man.' He says, 'Hello, Wiley.' You say, 'Hairy Man, I hear you're about the best conjure man around here.' 'I reckon I am.' You say, 'I bet you can't turn yourself into no giraffe.' You keep telling him he can't and he will. Then you say, 'I bet you can't turn yourself into no alligator.' And he will. Then you say, 'Anyone can turn into something as big as a man, but I bet you can't turn yourself into no possum.' When he does, you grab him and throw him in the sack."

"It don't sound right," said Wiley, "but I'll do it." He tied up his dogs so they wouldn't scare the Hairy Man away, and went down to the swamp again. He hadn't been there long when he saw the Hairy Man grinning through the trees. The Hairy Man knew Wiley had gone off without his hound dogs. Wiley nearly climbed a tree when he saw the croaker sack.

"Hello, Hairy Man," he said.

"Hello, Wiley." He took the sack off his shoulder and started to open it.

"Hairy Man, I hear you're the best conjure man around here."

"I reckon that's true."

"I bet you can't turn yourself into no giraffe."

"Shucks, that's easy."

"I bet you can't do it."

The Hairy Man twisted around and turned himself into a giraffe.

"I bet you can't turn yourself into an alligator."

The giraffe twisted around and turned into an alligator, all the time watching Wiley to see he didn't try to run off.

"Anybody can turn into something as big as a man," said Wiley, "but I bet you can't turn yourself into a possum."

The alligator twisted around and turned into a possum. Wiley grabbed the possum and threw it into the sack. He tied the sack up tight and then threw it into the river. But on his way home through the swamp, here come the Hairy Man again, grinning through the trees.

"I turned myself into the wind and blew out," he said. "Not I'm gonna sit right here until you get hungry and have to come down out of that bay tree."

Wiley thought for a while. He thought about the Hairy Man and about his hound dogs tied up almost a mile away.

"Well," he said, "you done some pretty smart tricks. But I bet you can't make things disappear and go where nobody knows."

"Yes, I can. Look at that old bird nest over there. Now look. It's gone."

"I didn't see any bird nest there. I bet you can't make something I know is there disappear."

"Ha!" said the Hairy Man. "Look at your shirt."

Wiley looked down and his shirt was gone.

"That was just a plain old shirt," he said, "but this rope I got tied round my britches has been conjured. I bet you can't make it disappear."

"Huh, I can make all the rope in this country disappear."

"Ha, ha, ha," laughed Wiley. "Bet you can't."

The Hairy Man looked mad. He opened his mouth wide and yelled out, "From now on all the rope in this country has disappeared."

Wiley held his britches with one hand and the tree limb with the other, and called out, "Hyeaaah, dog." He hollered loud enough to be heard in the next county.

When Wiley and the dogs got home he told his momma what had happened.

"Well, you fooled him twice. If you fool him again he has to leave you alone forever. He'll be mighty hard to fool the third time, though."

"We gotta find a way to fool him, Momma."

Wiley's momma sat down by the fire and held her chin between her hands and studied real hard. After a while, she said, "Wiley, go down to the pen and get that little suckin' pig away from the sow."

Wiley went and snatched the little pig through the rails and brought it back to his momma. She put it in his bed. "Now Wiley, you go on up to the loft and hide."

Before long he heard the wind howling and the trees shaking, and then the dogs started growling. He looked out through a knot-hole and saw the dog at the front door looking toward the swamp with his lips drawn back in a snarl.

Then a big animal with horns on its head ran out of the swamp toward the house. The dogs broke loose and took off after it.

"Oh, Lord," said Wiley, "the Hairy Man is coming here for sure."

Soon he heard something with feet like a cow scrambling around on the roof. He knew it was the Hairy Man because he heard him holler when he touched the hot chimney. The Hairy Man jumped off the roof and came up and knocked on the front door as big as you please.

"Wiley's momma! I done come after your baby!"

"You ain't gonna get him," momma hollered back.

"Give him here or I'll set your house on fire."

"I got plenty of water to put it out with."

"Give him here or I'll dry up your spring, make your cow go dry, and send a million boll weevils to eat up your cotton."

"Hairy Man, that's mighty mean."

"I'm a mighty mean man."

"If I give you my baby, will you go away from here and leave everything else alone?"

"I swear I will," said the Hairy Man. So momma opened the door and let him in.

"My baby's over there in that bed," she said.

The Hairy Man came in grinning. He stomped over to the bed and snatched the covers back.

"Hey," he hollered, "there ain't nothin' in this bed but a little suckin' pig."

"I ain't said what kind of baby I was givin' you."

The Hairy Man stomped, and raged, and gnashed his big teeth. Then he grabbed the pig and took off through the swamp, knocking down trees left and right. When the Hairy Man was gone, Wiley came down from the loft.

"Is he gone, Momma?"

"Yes, child. That old Hairy Man can never be back because we done fooled him three times."

Friends and Helpers

Anansi Saves Antelope

Doing a favor for a tiny creature eventually pays a big reward.

A bolt of lightning had started a fire. As it raged across the dry savanna, the animals panicked. Some were already surrounded by flames with no way to escape and others were running around frantically looking for a way to safety. While an antelope was looking for a way to escape she heard a tiny voice: "Please let me sit in your ear so you can carry me out of here."

It was Anansi the Spider, and without waiting for an invitation, he jumped down from a branch and settled in the antelope's ear. There seemed to be fire everywhere, and the antelope had no idea of which way to go to avoid it. But the spider knew the way out, and he directed the antelope calmly and confidently: "Go to the left, now straight, now to the right . . . until the antelope's swift legs had carried them both to safety across streams and brooks.

When the fire was far behind them, the spider ran down to the ground along the antelope's leg. "Thank you very much," he said. "I am sure we will meet again."

Sometime later, the antelope gave birth to a little baby. Like all baby antelopes, it was defenseless and spent most of its first few weeks hidden in the shrubs. Later, it could be seen grazing beside its mother. One day, two hunters spotted the mother antelope. While the little one crouched down under the shrubs, the mother leaped up to catch the hunters' attention, and then ran off, staying just out of range of their arrows. After an hour the hunters gave up the chase, and went back to look for the baby antelope. Though they were sure they were searching in the right place, they eventually left the forest empty handed.

Much later, the mother came back. She, too, searched for the baby but could not find it. Then she heard a familiar voice calling her. It was the spider. Anansi led her to a thicket surrounded by a dense spider web. While the hunters had been chasing the mother, Anansi had been very busy weaving webs that had kept the baby invisible—and safe—from the hunters.

The Ant and the Pigeon

An ant is saved by a pigeon, and almost immediately returns the favor.

One day an ant found a grain of corn and decided to take it home. He held it very tight, and hurried as fast as he could, so that nothing would take the grain of corn from him. There was a pond on the way home, but the ant, in its haste, had forgotten about it, and he fell in, corn and all.

The corn slipped from his mouth and went to the bottom of the pond. The ant stayed on top of the water and worked hard to find a place to get out. But after a while, the ant began to be afraid that his strength was about exhausted.

A pigeon came to the pond to drink, and she saw the ant struggling desperately. She decided that she would help the little fellow. She took a long, dry piece of grass and dripped it so that it fell near the ant. He climbed on to the grass and soon got out. The ant caught his breath, and then thanked the pigeon for saving him.

There was a boy near the pond with a bow and arrow. The ant saw him creeping up nearer and nearer to the pigeon. Hurrying as fast as he could, the ant climbed up the boy's leg and gave him a hard bite. The boy dropped his bow and arrow and cried out, and the pigeon saw him and flew to safety.

Each had saved the other. When the pigeon saved the ant she did not know that the ant would ever be able to do anything for her in return. Each was happier because of what each did for the other.

The Bura people say, "Every person is another's butter." Even a small person can do something for a great person.

Badger and Otter are Friends

Otter and Badger's friendship is tested when they let anger and hurt feelings keep them apart.

Badger and Otter became friends. "Let's exchange gifts as a mark of our friendship," suggested Badger. "I will bring you fresh honey every day."

"How nice," said Otter. "And I will catch a fish for you every day."

They soon were dear friends and visited each other all the time.

One day while Badger was collecting some honey, he met Tsuro, the hare.

"Where are you going?" asked the nosy hare.

"I am going to visit my good friend, Otter," answered Badger.

The next day Tsuro saw Otter on the path and asked where he was going.

"I am going to visit my dear friend, Badger," he answered.

Now, Tsuro was very annoyed because no one came to visit him. To himself he said, "I will break up this friendship."

The next day Tsuro saw Badger on his way to Otter's house with some honey. The hare ran ahead, hid near Otter's house, and watched. When Badger got closer, he called out, "You, Badger, do you hear me?"

"Who is that?" asked Badger.

"It is I, Otter," said the deceitful hare. "Do you know that my wife and children are ill from eating your wretched honey every day?"

Badger came nearer, intending to enter the house, but Tsuro shouted, "Go back. Don't come here again with your honey."

Badger asked, "My friend, why do you speak to me this way?"

"I told you. Your honey has made us sick. I do not want you to bring honey here any more."

So Badger went away and he was very angry.

The hare ran home quickly, and when he saw Badger coming, he asked, "Have you come back already? Was your friend not at home?"

"I do not wish to speak about him," Badger said. "He does not want my honey. He has insulted me. The friendship is over."

Then Tsuro said, "I would love to have your honey. Please give it to me and let us be friends."

Badger gave it to him, saying, "It is too heavy for me to carry home," and went on his way. When he got home, he told his wife and children what had happened.

The next day Otter caught a beautiful fish and started on his way with it to Badger's house. He said to himself, "I wonder why my friend did not come to see me yesterday? Maybe there is someone sick at his house. I had better go and see." He passed Tsuro's home, but the hare had run ahead and sat, hidden, waiting, near Badger's house.

"Where are you going, Otter?" asked the hare.

"I am going to your house," answered Otter, thinking he was talking to Badger.

"You had better not enter my house with your fish," shouted the hare. "One of my children has been much hurt by a bone from eating your fish. I do not want your old fish." Now Otter was angry, and he headed back home.

When Otter passed Tsuro's house, the hare called out, "What, back so soon? Did you not find your friend at home?"

"He insulted me greatly and that is why I am going home," replied Otter. Then the hare said, "Give me the fish and let us be friends." So Otter gave him the fish and went home.

Thereafter, Badger and Otter stayed at home and did not visit each other any more. But one day as Badger went to get honey, he met Otter on the road and said to him, "You are a bad fellow, Otter. You insulted me greatly the day I came to your house bringing you honey."

"I did not insult you," said Otter.

"Who was it then?" asked Badger.

"I do not know, but I was insulted at your house," said Otter.

"I am certain I never insulted you," said Badger.

"Well, then, let us renew our friendship and visit each other again," they both cried. Thus they became friends again.

When Tsuro saw Otter on his way to Badger's house, he said to him, "Why do you go to visit someone who insulted you?"

"I want to hear more about that matter," replied Otter, and continued on his way.

Hearing that, Tsuro ran ahead and sat hidden, awaiting him.

"Do you dare to come here again?" cried the hare to Otter. "My children have hardly recovered from the injuries they received from the fish bones. Why do you come again?"

Otter replied, "Stand there, my friend. I am coming to you."

The hare called out, "If you come here, I shall certainly beat you."

"Very well, but I am coming."

When Tsuro saw Otter coming towards him, he ran away.

As Otter could not find anyone, he called out, "Who was talking here?"

When Badger heard this, he came out of his house. "To whom are you talking?" he asked.

"Someone was here, insulting me," Otter replied, "but I do not know where he has gone."

"Let us search for his tracks and see who it was," said Badger.

They found Tsuro's footprints, and followed them to his house. When they reached the hare's house, Tsuro's wife told them her husband was very ill.

"How can he be ill?" said Otter. "I just passed him a little while ago and he was quite well. I want to see him and find out why he insulted me."

"Oh, please, come tomorrow," pleaded Tsuro's wife. "He is really so ill."

Thereupon, the two went away. During the night, Tsuro removed his home, and the next morning, when the two friends returned, everything was gone. "He is the one who tried to break up our friendship," said Otter. "He better never show his face around here again," said Badger. And he never did.

Help From Lightning

The Alur people, who live on the shore of Lake Albert, believe that nature comes to the aid of some people.

Two boys lived in the same village. They were the same age and liked to hunt and explore together. One day they went into the bush and set snares to catch birds. The first boy was lucky—he caught a pigeon. The second boy was unlucky—he only caught a spider. Feeling sorry for the tiny spider, he let it go.

The next day they went into the bush again to set snares. Once more the first boy was lucky—he caught a fat guinea fowl which is delicious to eat. But the second boy was unlucky—he caught only a stray bolt of lightning which he also released.

The following day, both boys were called before the king. He wanted some new grinding stones—large flat stones that are used to grind grain. Cutting a grinding stone is a difficult job, and is usually done by professional stone-cutters who have to chop the stone directly out of the rock.

Wondering what they were going to do, the two boys went out to a quarry near the village. They tried their best to cut some stones, but all they succeeded in doing was blunting the blades on their axes. The boys were becoming frightened. They knew the king would be angry if they failed to do what he had asked.

In desperation, the unlucky boy remembered the lightning he had released—maybe it would help. "Lightning!" he called. "I freed you from my snare, and now I need your help. Please come and cut some grinding stones for me."

Suddenly the sky flashed. Bolts of lightning struck the rock face. Sparks of fire and pieces of rock continued to fly in all directions until a pile of perfectly shaped grinding stones lay on the ground before the boys.

All the people in the village heard the thunder and saw the flashes of lightning. They came hurrying to see what had happened. They were amazed to see the pile of grinding stones, and helped the boys carry them to the king.

The king was very pleased with the two boys, but now he had an even more difficult task for them.

"Bring me a star from the sky," he commanded. No one had ever done such a thing before, and the boys had no idea how to go about this task. Then the unlucky boy remembered the spider he had released from his snare—maybe he would help.

"Spider! I freed you from my snare. Now I need your help. Please bring me a star from the sky."

The spider heard the boy's call for help. It spun an enormous web which reached from earth to sky. Then it climbed up into the sky and plucked a star which it then dragged back down to earth. The boys brought the star to the king.

Needless to say, the king was delighted. He was especially pleased with the second boy who had seemed so unlucky, but who had managed to achieve such wonderful success.

The boy was rewarded with many cows and baskets of food. He became wealthy and respected, and his advice was often sought by the other villagers.

The Man and the Bird

A poor man's wishes will forever be granted, if he can only
keep the cause of his good fortune a secret.

Long ago, there lived a poor man and his wife. Having no possessions, the husband
was obliged to search the forest for the food they ate. Often, it would mean a meal
of roots and berries, but sometimes he was fortunate enough to catch a bird or
animal in one of the traps and snares he set along the trails.

There was, however, a very large and beautiful bird which, although he saw it every-
day, had proved too clever to be enticed into even his most carefully hidden traps. Besides
this, it seemed to mock him as it remained just out of range of his bow and arrow, so that
eventually he determined that, come what may, he would capture it.

He was just about to return home empty-handed and hungry late one afternoon when
he remembered a trap he had forgotten to check. He retraced his steps and, upon reach-
ing it, gave a shout of joy for there, securely caught by a leg, was the lovely creature that
had fooled him so often.

He rushed forward, and seizing the bird by the neck said, "Today I have got you, my
friend!" whereupon he took out his knife and prepared to kill it, thankful that he would
have at least something, if only a bird, to take back to his wife that evening.

"Mercy, human, mercy!" cried the poor creature, as the grip upon its throat tightened. "Spare my life, and you have my word that you will not regret your kindness."

The man loosened his grasp and stepped back in surprise, the better to view the rare, golden-plumaged creature that addressed him, while it continued to speak. "Although my only earthly possessions are these golden feathers that cover me," said the bird, "yet in them lies a magic that will provide you with both food and drink for ever more. Release me, good human, for the thongs that hold me have eaten most painfully into my flesh."

Now, this was a difficult situation for the man. What if the bird was tricking him? He would lose the only food that he and his wife might have for several days. And yet, the bird itself might also have a wife—and maybe even babies—waiting anxiously for its return, also hungry, and hoping for food.

Then again, what if the bird spoke the truth? Why, he would be able to sit back in idleness for ever more! Such would be riches beyond counting. Besides, who had ever heard of a bird that spoke? He decided that he would risk it, and he untied the thong that had bitten so deeply into the poor creature's leg.

Thankfully the lovely bird stretched its aching limbs then, carefully pulling a golden-colored feather from each wing, gave them to the man. "With this gift, human," it said, "I also give you words of warning: if you wish to retain the magic properties of these feathers, you must neither speak nor boast to others of your good fortune. Should you do so, the power of my gift will vanish, and you will be left as poor as you are today. Therefore, do not treat my warning lightly. Wish as you hold these feathers in your hands, and they will fulfill your every desire."

The man thanked the bird for its gift and hastened home, wishing as he hurried along the path that he would find food in plenty waiting for him when he arrived. Which would he find, he wondered—starvation, or plenty?

The golden bird was as good as its word, for inside his hut the food vessels were overflowing, and the dried-up spring nearby gushed forth its sparkling waters once more, sparing his wife her daily walk to a water hole many miles away. Life smiled upon the couple at last. The husband was able to idle the days away, wishing for all the things that made life sweet, which came to him in abundance.

On many occasions the wife questioned her husband as to how it came about that though he no longer hunted in the forest, yet she always found food in her cooking pots, and luxuries besides? But each time she questioned him, the man avoided an explanation.

At last, as so often happens when life becomes too easy, the man grew careless of what he said, boasting to all around of his wealth, so that the woman grew increasingly suspicious of their good fortune. "Husband," she said, "you show no signs of astonishment at our wealth. You must be hiding something from me. Maybe at night while I sleep, you steal the good things that I find cooking upon the fire. Or perhaps you have secret dealings with 'the evil one' to bring sparkling water bubbling from the parched earth, when all else is dry! I must ask the witch-doctor to satisfy my mind upon these two matters."

Now, the very mention of witch-doctor struck terror into the heart of her simple husband, who had no wish for dealings with things he did not understand. "Wife," he begged, "do not call such a one, for by his arts he will surely find the magic feathers that provide us with all the good things that I bring."

Too late the man remembered the parting warning of the bird, as he realized that not only had he now shared his secret with his wife, but that he had boasted to others of his riches. It was with a deep foreboding that he held the feathers and wished his daily wishes on the following day, and his worst fears were confirmed—all his wishes remained unfulfilled and, on hastening to his bubbling spring, he found only drying mud.

Once more the couple felt the pangs of hunger, and the husband was obliged to reset his traps along the paths of the forest as of old. Life was harder, even than before, for the prolonged drought made food even harder to find. However, one day while visiting his traps as usual, he met a neighbor with his dog. "Let us hunt together," said Wanjobi, pleased to have company as he continued upon his rounds. To his great surprise they found the same golden bird, caught in one of the particularly well-hidden snares.

The husband rushed towards it exclaiming, "Once more you are in my power, oh golden bird, for I have caught you again! Give me two more of your magic feathers, and I will release you."

"Spare my life yet a second time, good human!" begged the bird, as he at once untied the noose that held it. But no sooner had he loosened the poor creature, than the neighbor's dog pounced upon it. Dragging the animal away with difficulty, the husband hastily picked up the bird and, running to the edge of the forest he released it, not waiting for his payment of the precious golden feathers.

"Once more, human, I thank you," said the bird gratefully. "But for your timely help, the dog would have killed me. In the past I made you a gift of my magic feathers because you spared my life when you and your wife were hungry, but there was a condition with my giving. You have suffered for not listening to my warning, and maybe you have learned your lesson.

"This time I will give you all that is within my power to give, and I make no condition with my gift. The magic in these feathers will last forever, for you have not only spared my life again—you have saved it. Also, you have trusted my word on two occasions."

Then, plucking two more feathers, one from each wing, the bird gave them to the man. Then, spreading its golden wings, the bird rose up into the heavens, and was gone.

It was a very happy man who returned to his wife that day. But he also never forgot that his failure to listen to his benefactor's warning had brought about his earlier downfall.

Hawk and Chicken Tales

Why Hawks Kill Chickens

When a hen's parents cannot afford to return her dowry payment, the king decrees that the hawk, who has been wronged, has the right to eat chickens whenever he pleases.

Once there was a very fine young hen who lived with her parents in the bush. One day a hawk was hovering round, about eleven o'clock in the morning, as was his custom, making large circles in the air and scarcely moving his wings. His keen eyes were wide open, taking in everything—for nothing moving ever escapes the eyes of a hawk, no matter how small it may be or how high up in the air the hawk may be circling.

This hawk saw the pretty hen picking up some corn near her father's house. He therefore closed his wings slightly, and in a flash was close to the ground. Then, spreading his wings out to check his flight, he alighted close to the hen and perched himself on the fence—as a hawk does not like to walk on the ground if he can help it.

He then greeted the young hen with his most enticing whistle, and offered to marry her. She agreed, so the hawk spoke to her parents, and paid the agreed amount of dowry, which consisted mostly of corn. The next day he returned, and took the young hen off to his home.

Shortly after this, a young cock who lived near the young hen's former home found out where she was living, and having been in love with her for some time—in fact, ever since his spurs had grown—determined to try and make her return to her own country. Therefore, at dawn, first having flapped his wings once or twice, he crowed in his best voice to the young hen. When she heard the sweet sound of the cock, she could not resist

his invitation. She quickly went out to him, and together they walked off to her parent's house, the young cock strutting in front, crowing proudly at intervals.

The hawk, who was hovering high up in the sky, quite out of sight of any ordinary eye, saw what had happened, and was furious. He made up his mind at once that he would obtain justice from the king, and flew off to Calabar, where he told the whole story, and asked for immediate redress.

The king sent for the parents of the hen, and told them they must repay to the hawk the dowry they had received from him on the marriage of their daughter, which was according to the custom. But the hen's parents said that they were so poor that they could not possibly afford to pay. So the king told the hawk that he could eat any of the cock's children whenever and wherever he found them as payment of his dowry, and, if the cock made any complaint, the king would not listen to him.

Hawk's Gift from the King

Hawks have a good reason for choosing chickens
as their favorite food.

During the reign of the king of Calabar, it was customary for rulers to give big feasts, to which all the subjects—the birds of the air and animals of the forest, and the things that lived in the water—were invited. The king always used the hawk—his favorite messenger—to deliver the invitations.

The hawk had served the king faithfully for many years, and finally was ready to retire. In gratitude for his long service, the king told the hawk to bring any living creature, bird or animal, to him, and after seeing it, he would allow the hawk to live on that particular species in the future.

The hawk then flew over the forests until he found a young owl which had tumbled out of its nest. This the hawk brought to the king, who agreed that the hawk had his permission to eat owls. The hawk then carried the owlet away, and told his friends what the king had said.

One of the wisest of the hawk's friends said, "Tell me, when you seized the young owlet, what did the parents say?" The hawk replied that the father and mother owls kept quiet, and never said anything. The hawk's friend then advised him to return the owlet to his parents, as he could never tell what the owls would do to him in the nighttime, and as they had made no noise, they surely must be plotting some dreadful reprisal.

The next day the hawk carried the owlet back to his parents and left him near the nest. He then flew about, trying to find some other bird which would do as his food; but as all the birds had heard that the hawk had seized the owlet, they hid themselves, and would not come out when he was near.

As he was flying home, he saw some fowls near a house, basking in the sun and scratching in the dust. There were also several small chickens running about and chasing insects, and an old hen clucking and calling to them from time to time.

The hawk decided that he would take a chicken, so he swooped down and caught the smallest one in his strong claws. Immediately, the cocks began to make a great noise, and the hen ran after him, with her feathers fluffed out, calling loudly for him to drop her child. But he carried it off, and all the fowls and chickens at once ran screaming around the yard, some taking shelter under bushes and others trying to hide themselves in the tall grass. He then carried the chicken to the king, telling him that he had returned the owlet to its parents, as he did not want him for food. The king told the hawk that for the future he could always feed on chickens.

The hawk then took the chicken home, and his friend who dropped in to see him, asked him what the parents of the chicken had done when they saw their child taken away.

"They all made a lot of noise," said the hawk, "and the old hen chased me, but nothing really happened."

His friend then said that it would now be quite safe to eat chickens, as the people who made plenty of noise in the daytime would go to sleep at night and not do him any injury. The only people to be afraid of were those who when they were injured, kept quite silent. You might be certain that they were plotting mischief, and would get revenge the first chance they got.

The Missing Ring

A ring is necessary for a wedding ceremony, but the one the hawk had made for his bride is missing.

The hawk was ready to get married. He traveled about from one village to another until at last he found the right girl. He spoke to the girl's father, and all of the arrangements were made. After setting the date for the wedding, the hawk returned home.

He gathered all the gold dust he had saved and took it to a goldsmith to have a ring made. Because the hawk was so handsome, some creatures envied him and said unkind things behind his back. Not everyone wished him well.

When the day of the wedding was near, the hawk went to the goldsmith to get the ring for his bride. Then he called for his friends to accompany him to her village. His friend the lizard came. His friend the guinea fowl came. And so did his friends mantis and snake. Many others from his village also joined the wedding party.

They went to the house of the girl the hawk had chosen. The hawk introduced his friends to the girl's family, and the celebration began. After much drumming and singing, the hawk put his hand in his pocket for the ring. But the ring was not there. He searched through his clothes, but the ring could not be found.

At last he cried out, "The ring has been stolen!"

The headman of the village said, "Let everyone be searched."

So everyone in the village was searched, but the ring was not found.

The hawk approached the girl's father. "I took all the gold dust I had been saving," he said, "and I had a most beautiful ring made. I brought it with me, but someone who does not wish me well has stolen it from my pocket."

The father of the girl said, "Everyone has been searched but the ring has not been found. Though you have an explanation, the fact remains—there is no ring. Therefore, the wedding cannot take place. When you return with the ring, we will talk of the matter again."

The hawk was overcome with shame. His friends, too, were ashamed. The lizard was speechless—he could only move his head from side to side as if to say, "Oh, what a terrible thing!"

The guinea fowl clapped his hands violently against his head, saying, "Disgrace, disgrace!"

The mantis kept hitting his sides with his fists, saying "Oh, no, it cannot be true!"

And the snake opened his mouth, and put out his tongue, turning this way and that to show everyone that he did not have the ring there.

The hawk and his friends went away. "I will search for the person who stole the ring," the hawk said. He flew into the air and soared over the countryside, looking for the thief.

As for the lizard, he has never spoken a word since that day. He simply moves his head from side to side as if to say, "Oh, what a terrible thing!" Because the guinea fowl repeatedly clapped his hands so hard against his head, his head became bald, and so it remained. Because the mantis struck his sides so hard with his fists, he became very thin. And whenever the snake meets someone, he opens his mouth and puts his tongue out to show that he does not have the ring hidden there.

The hawk has never given up the search. He forever soars and hovers in the sky, diving down now and then upon some moving creature to see if it is wearing the missing ring.

Rabbit Stories

Because Southern blacks drew much of their story material from the barnyard, fields and woods which made up their environment, forest creatures had a significant role in their stories. Brer (a contraction of "Brother") Rabbit, the popular trickster character who appears throughout so much of the African-American folklore, is the rascal who never tires of concocting deceptions and hoaxes. But just why the rabbit and the fox were so often featured in the stories, instead of the more familiar coon and possum, remains a mystery.

Who Ate the Butter?

Not only does Rabbit get out of doing any work, but he eats all the food out of Fox's icebox and then blames the theft on Bear.

The Fox had a big plantation and the rest of the animals were all working for him. Fox had them all chopping weeds out of the cornfield. Soon, Rabbit gets tired and wants to fool around so he starts thinking of an excuse to get away. But Fox had Bear overseeing for him, and Bear was pretty tough on Rabbit because he knew Rabbit was shiftless—just lollygagging around and doing nothing all day.

Well, pretty soon Rabbit calls Bear over and tells him he's going to have to take about an hour off. Bear wants to know what for, and Rabbit says his wife is about to have a baby and needs his help.

Bear says okay, and Rabbit skeddadles real fast. Then he looks around for some mischief to get into, and finally has an idea. He's all tired and hungry, and he knows that Fox has gone into the city, so Rabbit decides to go over to Fox's house. He looks in the icebox, finds some fried chicken and fruit, and eats it up. Then he skips out into the shrubs and rests until he notices the hour is about up.

When Rabbit gets back to the field everyone wants to know what he named the baby. The first thing that comes into Rabbit's mind is all the food in the icebox, which he wants to get back to, so he said, "Number One Gone."

Rabbit begins to work again, but the more he works the more he's thinking about that food still in the icebox, and how he can get back to it. Well, rabbits have more than one baby at a time, so he calls Bear back and tells him, "It's about time, Mr. Bear."

"Time for what?" asks Bear.

"Time for my wife to have another baby," said Rabbit.

Bear let him go again, and Rabbit made a beeline for the icebox. He started on some ham, and didn't stop till it was all gone.

When Rabbit gets back to the field the others want to know what he named the second baby. Rabbit tells them, "Number Two Gone." Then Rabbit starts working again, while everyone else is wondering why he gave his babies such odd names.

After about an hour, Rabbit calls Bear over again with the same excuse, and then makes another beeline for Fox's icebox. This time he eats up all the beef—he can only eat so much at one time, you know. When he gets back he tells everyone that this baby's name is "Half Gone."

After working maybe a half hour, Rabbit says he has to take another leave of absence. He hurries over to Fox's icebox, drinks up all the juice and milk he can hold, and goes back to the field.

"What's this one's name?" they want to know.

"Three Fourths Gone," says Rabbit.

Rabbit works a little bit longer and then says he has to go again. This time he drinks up all the cream, and eats all the cheese and butter. When he gets back to the field he tells everyone, "Well, that's the last baby and I named him 'All Gone.'"

Late in the afternoon, Fox comes back from town, driving in his big Cadillac out to the field. "What's been goin' on while I was gone?" he says. "Someone ate up all my food."

"Well, everyone's been here all day except for Brother Rabbit," said Bear, "and I really don't think he had time to do it because he's been helping his wife have her babies."

"Well, when everyone gets in camp tonight, I'll find out who done it," said Fox.

That night Fox arranged for a big barbecue. After working hard all day, and then eating so much barbecue, everyone is just exhausted and they go right to sleep. While they're sleeping, Fox builds a great big fire. He knows that the heat from the fire will make the butter run out of whoever ate it. But Fox was drowsy, too, and while he was sitting up waiting to see who the butter was coming out of, he fell asleep.

For some reason, Rabbit woke up and saw a pool of butter all around him—and he knew what Fox was up to. He rubbed the butter all over Bear and then tiptoed down to the pond and washed himself off—not a speck of butter was left on him. When he got back to camp, everybody was sound asleep and the fire was still going. Soon, Rabbit's fur was all fluffy and dry. Rabbit picked up a little pebble, threw it at Fox to wake him up, and then laid down and pretended he was asleep.

Fox wakes up and decides it's time to examine everyone while they're still asleep. Since Rabbit was the only one that left the field that day, he thought he should check him first. But Rabbit was all dry.

"Bear's the biggest and best able to eat two pounds of butter," thought Fox, "so I'll check him next." Sure enough, Bear was covered with butter.

Rabbit, who was watching everything, knew Fox was headed to the house to get his shotgun. He lay real quiet, just watching. When Fox was almost within shooting distance of Bear, Rabbit wakes Bear up and tells him Fox is going to shoot him for eating up all his food. Bear is all surprised and confused and wants to argue about it, but Rabbit tells him, "You better run."

"I don't have anything to run for," says Bear.

"You just wait a minute more and you'll have something to run for," says Rabbit.

Just then, Fox sees Bear standing up and figures he's trying to get away, and lets both barrels loose.

"Well, Brother Bear, I guess you got something to run for now," says Brother Rabbit.

Bear cut out through the thicket while Fox was reloading, and the two of them went running—Bear with Fox shooting at him.

Rabbit tells Fox he'll help catch Bear, but instead he runs off and hides. After a while, Fox loses sight of Bear and gives up the chase.

Pretty soon, Rabbit catches up with Bear and says, "I told you so, I told you Fox was going to kill you for eating up all his food."

"But, Brother Rabbit, I swear I didn't do it," says Bear.

"It don't make no difference," says Rabbit. "He's going to kill you anyway because you know you'll never change his mind."

Bear was so upset. "What should I do?" he asked Rabbit.

"Well if I were you, I'd go to some other part of the woods," advised Rabbit, "because you definitely can't live around here anymore."

And that's what Bear did.

Rabbit couldn't have been more pleased with himself. He skipped back to Fox's house. Fox was sitting on his front porch with his shotgun across his lap—just in case Bear came back and tried to soft-talk him. But Rabbit told Fox he didn't have anything to worry about any more.

"How come?" said Fox.

"Because I chased Bear into some quicksand," said Rabbit.

Fox was so grateful he made Rabbit his new foreman, and no one ever heard from Bear again.

The Hare, the Hippo, and the Elephant

The hippo and elephant may be big and strong, but that doesn't mean anything when it comes to dealing with a very smart hare.

The hare was splashing around in the river when he met the hippo. "My, my, you surely look strong," said the hare to the hippo. "Do you think if I tied myself to you and went into the bush, you could pull me into the river?"

"Certainly I could pull you into the river," snorted the hippo. "That would be very easy, for you are but a little thing."

"Well, we will see about that," the hare said to himself.

To the hippo he said, "Very well, then. When you feel a tug on the rope, start pulling."

The hare tied one end of the rope to the hippo. Holding the other end of the rope, he ran into the bush where he met the elephant.

"Hello, elephant," said the hare. "You surely look strong. Do you think if I tied this rope to you, you could pull me out of the river?"

"Well, of course, I could!" said the elephant. "That would be easy, for you are but a very small thing." And so the hare tied the other end of the rope around the elephant.

"When I get to the water, I will tug on the rope, and you can start pulling," the hare said to the elephant.

The hare hurried out of sight, tugged on the rope, and ran off. The elephant began to pull at one end, and the hippo at the other. The hippo said, "How can that little hare be so strong?"

Likewise, the elephant said, "How can I be pulling for so long against such a tiny creature?"

When the two had been tugging at each other for a long time, the hippo left the river to find the hare, and the elephant headed to the river to do the same. The two were very surprised when they met.

"Is it you, my friend, who has been pulling?" the hippo said to the elephant.

The other replied, "Is it you who has been pulling at the other end?" Thereupon they became friends.

After that the hippo always came on land to eat grass, and the elephant went to the river to drink water.

Granny, Cutta the Cord

Brer Wolf should know not to trust Brer Rabbit,
but somehow he never learns his lesson.

One time food got very scarce. The rice crop was poor. Fish were swimming too low to catch and birds were flying too high to shoot. It was really very hard times and all the animals were mighty hungry. Brer Rabbit and Brer Wolf put their heads together to figure out what to do.

After a while, Brer Rabbit, weeping bitter tears, said the only thing left to do was to eat their grandmothers. Brer Wolf just wailed. Brer Rabbit said, "If you're going to take it so hard, Brer Wolf, it would be better for you to kill your grandmother first and get it over with. That way you'll be done with your grieving faster."

So Brer Wolf dried his eyes and killed his grandmother. Then he and Brer Rabbit went off and they ate and ate day and night until the food was all gone. Soon after, Brer Wolf went visiting Brer Rabbit and said, "Brer Rabbit, I am hungry through and through. It's time to kill your grandmother now so we can have something to eat."

Brer Rabbit threw back his head and burst out laughing. "You think I'm going to kill my own grandmother?" he said. "Oh no, Brer Wolf, I could never do that."

This made Brer Wolf so mad he tore at his hair with his claws and howled. He said he was going to make Brer Rabbit kill his grandmother somehow.

That night, Brer Rabbit took his grandmother by the hand and led her way off into the woods. He hid her at the top of a huge coconut tree and told her to stay there quietly. Then he gave her a little basket with a cord tied to it so that he could send food up to her.

The next morning, Brer Rabbit went to the foot of the tree, and hollered in a fine voice:

Granny, granny, o granny! Cutta the cord.

When the grandmother heard this, she let down the basket with the cord, and Brer Rabbit filled it with things to eat. Every day he came back and did the same thing, and every day she let down the basket.

Brer Wolf watched and listened. He crept up close and bye and bye he heard what Brer Rabbit was saying, and he saw the basket swing down on the cord and go back up again. When Brer Rabbit left, Brer Wolf sneaked up to the foot of the tree and said:

Granny, granny, o granny! Shoota the cord.

Old Granny Rabbit listened closely. She said, "What's happening here? My grandson doesn't talk like that." When Brer Rabbit came back to see his grandmother, she told him about how someone was hollering "shoota the cord." Brer Rabbit just laughed until he couldn't laugh anymore.

When Brer Rabbit went away, Brer Wolf came back to the tree and hollered:

Granny, granny, o granny! Cutta the cord.

Granny Rabbit held her head to one side and listened hard. "I'm sorry, my son, that you have such a bad cold. Your voice is sounding very hoarse." Then she peeked through the branches and saw Brer Wolf. "You can't fool me," she said. "Go away now, you hear?"

Brer Wolf snorted and gnashed his teeth, and stomped off into the swamp to think about his problem. Bye and bye, he went to the blacksmith and asked him how he could make his voice less hoarse-sounding, so that it could sound fine like Brer Rabbit's.

The blacksmith said, "I can run this hot poker down your throat and then you'll be able to talk nice and easy like Brer Rabbit." Well, it hurt real bad and it was a long time before Brer Wolf could talk at all, but he finally walked back to that coconut tree. When he got there he hollered:

Granny, granny, o granny! Cutta the cord.

The voice sounded so nice and fine to Granny Rabbit that she was sure it was Brer Rabbit. She let down the basket and Brer Wolf climbed in. Then Granny Rabbit started to pull on the cord.

"Lord, this load is heavy," she said. "My grandson must be sending me an awful lot of food this time."

Brer Wolf couldn't help grinning when he heard her say this, but he kept real still. Granny Rabbit pulled hard. She pulled until she got so tired she had to rest, leaving Brer Wolf dangling way up high in the air. Brer Wolf was up so high that when he looked down he got dizzy. When he looked up, though, his mouth started to water. Then he looked down again and he saw Brer Rabbit. That scared Brer Wolf and he jerked on the rope a little.

Brer Rabbit got to the bottom of the coconut tree and hollered:

Granny, granny, o granny! Cutta the cord.

Granny Rabbit cut the cord on the basket and Brer Wolf fell to the ground and never bothered anyone else again.

Rabbit's Horse

The most outrageous scheme is okay with Rabbit
if it will get him what he wants.

A very long time ago, Rabbit and Tiger were best friends. But when they discovered that they both were courting the same young lady, they became very jealous of each other.

Well, you know Rabbit—always looking to get the advantage. One day, he goes over to the young lady's house and, as usual, starts bragging on himself, and telling her that Tiger wasn't anything but his father's old riding horse. A little later, Tiger stopped by to call on this girl he thought was his sweetheart. But she said, "Go on now! How can you just come along courting when I just heard you are nothing but an old riding horse?"

"What?" said Tiger. "Whoever told you such a thing is making up stories about me and filling your head with big lies. Tell you what I'll do. I'll go straight to my friend Rabbit, and he'll tell you that all of this is just nonsense. I never have been his father's old riding horse."

So Tiger took up his walking stick, and walking just as respectfully as he can, he goes straight to Rabbit's house. He found Rabbit lying there on his bed moaning with fever. So he lifted the latch and called out, "Brer Rabbit! Brer Rabbit!"

Rabbit heard him just fine, but he answered real soft and sicklike, "Brer Tiger, is that you calling me?" He knew that Tiger was going to be mad at him, you know.

Tiger said, "Yes, it's me. I came right over to your house because someone has been telling lies about me, and I wanted to find out if it was you. I want to hear it from your own mouth. If you said those things, I'm going to make you prove it."

"Oooh," Rabbit groaned. "Can't you see I have a fever? My stomach is hurting me bad, and I have just been to the doctor and taken some medicine."

"Is that so?" said Tiger. "I don't believe you."

"I just swallowed two pills, Brer Tiger, so how do you think I could ever get up and go to any lady's yard and prove anything tonight?"

"I don't want to have an argument," said Brer Tiger, "but I think you better come with me anyhow and tell that lady tonight that I am not your father's old riding horse."

"Oh, Lord!" cried Rabbit. "This pain in my chest just won't let me. But if you insist, I'll try to go with you even though I'm feeling so sick."

Then Tiger said, "Well, since you're so sick, maybe I could help you get there. How can I help?"

"Well, just lift me up a little and I'll see how I feel," said Rabbit.

So Tiger lifted him up and Rabbit said, "Oh, Lord! I'm feeling dizzy."

"Don't worry," said Tiger. "Just grab my neck and I'll carry you on my back."

But Rabbit insisted he couldn't get up at all. And every time that Tiger lifted him, he just fell back into bed. Finally, Rabbit looked up and said, "Why don't you get that saddle up there in the rafters and put it on, and I could maybe grab hold of that and you could carry me." So Tiger took down Brer Rabbit's saddle.

"Now, just put that on your back, brother," said Brer Rabbit, "and I can sit down soft."

Rabbit got in the saddle and then got his bridle and reins. "Hey!" said Tiger, "what are you going to do with that?"

Brer Rabbit said, "If you just put that through your mouth, brother, then I can tell you if you're going too fast so I won't fall off."

"All right, then, put it on," said Tiger.

Next Rabbit took out his whip. "Hey!" said Tiger, "what are you going to do with that?"

"If a fly comes on your ear or back, brother, I'll be able to take this whip and lick it off."

Tiger said, "Well, okay."

Then Rabbit put on his spurs. "Hey!" said Tiger. "Now what are you going to do with those?"

"If flies come on your side, brother, I can brush them away with my spurs."

"Okay, then. Put them on."

Then Rabbit moaned, "Well, Brer Tiger, if you stoop down, I can get on."

Rabbit mounted Tiger's back, and he started off. After about a mile or so, Rabbit took his whip and gave Tiger a lick on the ear. "Hey! What's that for?"

"Well, there was a fly on your ear. Shoo fly! Shoo!"

"All right, brother, but next time don't hit me so hard."

Tiger went on for another mile or so and Rabbit stuck his spurs in his side. Tiger jumped and cried out, "Now wait a minute! What do you think you're doing?"

"Those bothersome flies were biting your sides."

Tiger went on until he came to the lady's yard. The lady's house had two doors, a front one and a back one. Just as he came to the entrance to the yard, Rabbit rose up in his saddle just like a jockey on a race horse, and he took out his whip and he lashed Tiger hard!

"Hey!" cried Tiger. But Rabbit lashed him some more until he started to run. Then Rabbit took his spurs and stuck them into Tiger's side, and made him run right up to the lady's front door.

At the door, Rabbit took off his hat and waved it above his head. "Good morning, miss," he said. "Didn't I tell you that Tiger was nothing but my father's old riding horse?"

Rabbit hopped off Tiger and went into the lady's house. And poor Tiger was so embarrassed that he galloped off, and was never heard of again.

The Favorite Uncle Remus

JOEL CHANDLER HARRIS

No child could ever be better entertained than the little boy fortunate enough to be told stories by the man he called Uncle Remus.

THE WONDERFUL TAR BABY

Didn't the fox ever catch the rabbit, Uncle Remus?" asked the little boy the next morning.

He come mighty nigh it, honey, sho's you bawn—Brer Fox did. One day Brer went ter wuk en got 'im some tar, and mix it wid some turkentime, en fix up a contraption w'at he call a Tar-Baby en he set 'er in de big road, en den he lay off in de bushes fer to see w'at de news was gwineter be. En he didn't hatter wait long, needer, kaze bimeby yer come Brer Rabbit pacin' down de road—*lippity-clippity, clippity, lippity*—des ez sassy ez a jay-bird. Brer Fox, he lay low. Brer Rabbit come prancin' long till he spy de Tar-Baby, en den he fotch up on his behime legs like he wuz 'stonished. De Tar-Baby, she sot dar, she did, en Brer Fox, he lay low.

"Mawnin!" sez Brer Rabbit, sezee—"nice wedder dis mawnin," sezee.

Tar-Baby ain't sayin' nothin', en Brer Fox, he lay low.

"How does yo' sym'toms seem ter segashuate?" sez Brer Rabbit, sezee.

Brer Fox, he wink his eye slow, en lay low, en de Tar-Baby, she ain't sayin' nothin'.

"How you come on, den? Is you deaf?" sez Brer Rabbit, sezee. "Kaze if you is, I kin holler louder," sezee.

Tar-Baby stay still, en Brer Fox, he lay low.

"Youer stuck up, dat's w'at you is," sez Brer Rabbit, sezee, "en I'm gwineter cure you, dat's w'at I'm a-gwineter do," sezee.

Brer Fox, he sorter chuckle in his stomach, he did, but Tar-Baby ain't sayin' nothin'.

"I'm gwineter larn you how ter talk ter 'spectable folks ef hit's de las' ack," sez Brer Rabbit, sezee. "Ef you don't take off dat hat en tell me howdy, I'm gwineter bus' you wide open," sezee.

Tar-Baby stay still, en Brer Fox, he lay low.

Brer Rabbit keep on axin' 'im, en de Tar-Baby, she keep on sayin' nothin', till present'y Brer Rabbit draw back wid his fis', he did, en *blip* he tuck 'er side er de head. Right dar's whar he broke his merlasses jug. His fis' stuck, en he can't pull loose. De tar holt 'im. But Tar-Baby, she stay still, en Brer Fox, he lay low.

"Ef you don't lemme loose, I'll knock you agin," sez Brer Rabbit, sezee, en wid dat he fotch 'er a wipe wid de udder han', en dat stuck. Tar-Baby, she ain't sayin' nothin', en Brer Fox, he lay low.

"Tu'n me loose, fo' I kick de natal stuffin' outen you," sez Brer Rabbit, sezee, but de Tar-Baby, she ain't sayin' nothin'. She des hilt on, en den Brer Rabbit lose de use er his foots in de same way. Brer Fox, he lay low. Den Brer Rabbit squall out dat ef de Tar-Baby don't tu'n 'im loose he butt 'er cranksided. En den he butter, en his head got stuck. Den Brer Fox, he sa'ntered fort', lookin' des ez inner-cent ez one er yo' mammy's mockin'-birds.

"Howdy, Brer Rabbit," sez Brer Fox, sezee. "You look sorter stuck up dis mawnin'," sezee, en den he rolled on de groun', en laffed en laffed till he couldn't laff no mo'.

THE BRIAR PATCH

Uncle Remus, asked the little boy the next evening, did the fox kill and eat the rabbit when he caught him with the Tar-Baby?

"Law honey, w'at I tell you w'en I fus' begin? I tole you Brer Rabbit wuz a monstus soon creetur—leas'ways dat's w'at I laid out fer ter tell you. Well den, honey, don't you go en make no calkalations, kaze in dem days Brer Rabbit en his fambly wuz at de head er de gang w'en any racket wuz on han', en dar dey stayed. 'Fo' you begins fer ter wipe yo' eyes 'bout Brer Rabbit, you wait en see whar'bouts Brer Rabbit gwineter fetch up at.

W'en Brer Fox fine Brer Rabbit mixed up wid de Tar-Baby, he feel mighty good, en he roll on de groun' en laff. Bimeby he got up'n say, sezee:

"Well, I speck I got you dis time, Brer Rabbit, sezee; 'maybe I ain't, but I speck I is. You bin runnin' roun' here sassin' atter me a mighty long time, but I speck you done come ter de een' er de row. You bin cuttin' up yo' capers en bouncin' roun' in dis neighborhood till you come ter b'lieve yo'se'f de boss er de whole gang. En den youer allers some'rs whar you got no business," sez Brer Fox, sezee. "Who ax you fer ter come en strike up a'quain'tance wid dish yer Tar-Baby? En who stuck you up dar whar you is? Nobody in de roun' worril. You des tuck en jam yo'se'f on dat Tar-Baby widout waitin' fer any invite," sez Brer Fox, sezee, "en dar you is, en dar you'll stay till I fixes up a breshpile en fires her up, kaze I'm gwineter bobbycue you dis day, sho," sez Brer Fox, sezee.

Den Brer Rabbit talk mighty 'umble.

"I don't keer w'at you do wid me, Brer Fox," sezee, "so you don't fling me in dat briar-patch. Roas' me, Brer Fox," sezee, "but don't fling me in dat briar-patch," sezee.

"Hit's so much trouble fer ter kin'le a fire," sez Brer Fox, sezee, "dat I speck I'll hatter hang you," sezee.

"Hang me des ez high ez you please, Brer Fox," sez Brer Rabbit, sezee, "but do fer de Lord's sake don't fling me in dat briar-patch," sezee.

"I ain't got no string," sez Brer Fox, sezee, "en now I speck I'll hatter drown you," sezee.

"Drown me des eze deep ez you please, Brer Fox," sez Brer Rabbit, sezee, "but do don't fling me in dat briar-patch," sezee.

"Dey ain't no water nigh," sez Brer Fox, sezee, "en now I speck I'll hatter skin you," sezee.

"Skin me, Brer Fox," sez Brer Rabbit, sezee, "snatch out my eyeballs, t'ar out my years by de roots, en cut off my legs," sezee, "but please, Brer Fox, don't fling me in dat briar-patch," sezee.

Co'se Brer Fox wanter hu't Brer Rabbit bad ez he kin, so he kotch 'im by de behime legs en slung 'im right in de middle er de briar-patch. Dar wuz a consider'ble flutter whar Brer Rabbit struck de bushes, en Brer Fox sorter hang roun' fer ter see w'at wuz gwineter happen. Bimeby he year somebody call 'im, en way up de hill he see Brer Rabbit settin' cross-legged on a chinkapin log combin' de pitch outen his ha'r wid a chip. Den Brer Fox know dat he bin swop off mighty bad. Brer Rabbit wuz bleedz fer ter fling back some er his sass, en he holler out:

"Bred en bawn in a briar-patch, Brer Fox—bred en bawn in a briar-patch!" en wid dat he skip out des ez lively ez a cricket in de embers.

How Sandy Got His Meat

Thanks to Brer Rabbit, Brer Coon was able to catch enough frogs to feed his family for quite some time.

Brer Rabbit and Brer Coon were fishermen. Brer Rabbit fished for fish and Brer Coon fished for frogs.

After a while the frogs all got so smart Brer Coon couldn't catch them anymore. He hadn't brought any meat home for weeks. His children were hungry, and his wife was upset.

Brer Coon felt mighty bad and he was walking along the road with his head down wondering what he was going to do. Just then Brer Rabbit was skipping down the road. He could tell Brer Coon was worried, so he threw up his ears and said:

"Mornin', Brer Coon."

"Mornin', Brer Rabbit."

"How you doin', Brer Coon?"

"Poorly, Brer Rabbit, poorly. The frogs has all got so wiley I can't catch 'em, and I got no meat to my house and my wife is mad and the children is hungry. Brer Rabbit, I need help."

Old Brer Rabbit looked away across the river a long time. Then he scratched his ear with his hind foot and said:

"I'll tell you what we do, Brer Coon. We'll get every one of them frogs. You go down on the sand bar and lie down and play like you're dead. Don't move. No matter what, just stay still."

Old Brer Coon moseyed down to the river. The frogs heard him coming and the big frog said, "You better look round. You better look round."

Another frog said, "Knee deep, knee deep."

And *kerchung!* All the frogs went in the water.

But Brer Coon just laid down on the sand and stretched out just like he was dead. The flies got all over him, but he didn't move. The sun shone hot, but he didn't move.

Directly Brer Rabbit came running through the woods and out on the sand bar, and put his ears up high and hollered out:

"I don't bleve it. I don't bleve it!"

And all the little frogs around the edge said:

"I don't bleve it. I don't bleve it!"

But the old coon played like he was dead, and all the frogs came up out of the river and sat around where the old coon lay.

Just then Brer Rabbit winked his eye and said:

"I'll tell you what I'd do, Brer Frogs. I'd bury ole Sandy, bury him so deep he never could scratch out."

Then all the frogs started to dig out the sand from under the old coon. When they had dug a great, deep hole with the old coon in the middle of it, the frogs all got tired and the big frog said:

"Deep enough. Deep enough. Deep enough."

Brer Rabbit was taking a nap in the sun, and he woke up and said:

"Can you jump out?"

The big frog looked up to the top of the hole and said:

"Yes I can. Yes I can. Yes I can."

And the little frogs said:

"Yes I can. Yes I can. Yes I can."

Brer Rabbit said:

"Dig it deeper."

Liar, Fool, and Tall Tales

"Little boy," said the man, "have you a mother?"

"Yes, sir," said the boy.

"Where is she?"

"She has gone to the king's palace to sew it up with her needle and thread where it got torn last night."

"What!" exclaimed the man. "And where is your father?"

"He has gone to the river to get some water to throw on the land with a flower pot with a hole in it, to make a garden."

"Is that so?" said the man.

"Little boy, did you hear that a child was born last night with seven arms, seven legs, and seven necks?"

"Sir, I can't be sure, but this morning, when I went to the spring for water, I found a dress with seven sleeves and seven collars, and I think it must have belonged to that baby."

"Is that so?" said the man.

"Little boy, did you hear that a donkey took a journey into the sky last week?"

"Sir, I can't be sure, but when I went to the spring last week, I heard a clap of thunder, and when I looked up, I saw a pack saddle falling down from the sky, and I think it must have belonged to that donkey."

"Little boy, did you hear that last week the river caught fire?"

"Sir, I can't be sure, but last week when we went fishing, we caught a lot of fish burnt on one side and raw on the other. I think they must have been cooked when the river caught fire."

"My dear child, take my cow. You are the smartest little fellow I ever saw."

On his way home, the man met Mr. Wolf. "Why do you look so sad?" Mr. Wolf asked him.

"I thought I was the biggest liar in the world, so I said I would give my cow to anyone who could beat me lying. Then I met an innocent little child who told bigger lies than me, so I had to give him the cow. I don't know what to do to get the cow back from him."

"I'll go back with you," said Mr. Wolf. "I have seven bags here full of lies. If I open but one of my bags, the whole town will be covered with lies."

"All right," said the man. "Let's go."

When the little boy saw them coming towards his house, he knew they were going to try to take his cow. Before they got any closer, he called out, "How come you're only bringing one of the wolves you promised my father? Well, I guess he'll have to do. Bring him in and we'll cook him up."

"What?" cried Mr. Wolf. "Is that why you brought me?" And Mr. Wolf ran for home as fast as his legs would carry him.

"Sir, why are you still standing there?" asked the little boy. "If you wait, Mr. Wolf will steal the road and put it in his pocket, and then how will you get home?"

"What?" said the man, and he started running after Mr. Wolf to catch him before he stole the road and put it in his pocket.

The little boy never saw either one of them again. He went inside happy because he had his cow, and because he was the smartest little boy in the world.

"All right. Lily, run salt the puddin' please, honey."

"Can't. I'm looking high and low for my hair ribbon."

So Mrs. Simpson threw her dust rag across a chair back, washed her hands, and salted the puddin'.

Just about the time she got back to her dusting, Lily got to thinking how she should help her ma. So she hurried into the kitchen and salted the puddin'.

Lily had no more than got back to searching for her hair ribbon when Jenny got to feeling bad about being so sassy. So she ran down to the kitchen and salted the puddin'.

Bertha always was the queen of the family. She never did much more than lay around reading a romance novel, but if there was a thing she liked more than reading it was eating her ma's puddin'. So she went and salted it. She got to the kitchen just after Sara left.

Well, that puddin' sure baked pretty and when Mrs. Simpson carried it out that night you could just hear everybody sort of smack their lips.

The preacher was there, so naturally he got the first helping. His eyes were shining and he said something about nothing being better than Mrs. Simpson's puddin'. Then he took a whopping big mouthful.

When he bit down to kind of let the flavor soak in, his eyes squinched up and his mouth turned down. Then he asked for some water.

Well, everybody just sat there with their mouths open wide and their eyes bugged out. Mrs. Simpson sort of caught on that something was wrong, so she took a taste herself. Then she knew.

"Which one of you girls salted the puddin'?"

"I did, Ma," all five of them said together.

"And so did I," said their ma. "It sure looks like too many cooks spoiled this puddin'."

And nobody could deny it.

Biography

restrooms and houses of worship and public parks for blacks and for whites. The races played sports separately, sat in different parts of movie theaters, and ate in different sections of restaurants. Perhaps most important, they had very different views of history.

Longtime white residents of Richmond were proud of their battlefield memorials and their southern heritage. Many blacks knew little or nothing of their own history—their ancestors had been prevented from learning to read or write, taking the stories of their lives with them to the grave. Yet Arthur Ashe and his family were fortunate. Large, close, and inquisitive, they traced their roots back more than three hundred years to an African woman who survived the frightful voyage from the continent of her birth to Virginia on board an eighty-ton English ship known as *The Doddington*.

A West African, as were most slaves, the young woman was known only by a number until she was purchased by a man named Blackwell. She took the name of Blackwell and married a slave with that name. They had a daughter, Lucy, according to Virginia records. She was the first American-born member of Arthur Ashes's family tree. Several generations later, a person on the Blackwell side of the family married a South Carolina native who bore the name of Ashe, from an early governor of North Carolina. The Ashes had a son, Arthur, who married and became the tennis star's father.

How could the Ashe family know this? Fortunately, an aunt still keeps a huge family tree, painted on canvas, with the names of dozens of family members. Each is represented by a single leaf. The tree stands six by seven feet and was put together through years of careful research in old and musty courthouses along the East Coast. In the middle of the tree is a family crest showing a chain with a broken link. The broken chain symbolizes freedom for the slaves. Tennis star Arthur Ashe is the only person among fifteen hundred family members whose leaf is painted in gleaming gold.

Arthur certainly did not seem destined for stardom on July 10, 1943. He was a small, thin baby, and his lean appearance would stay with him all of his days. He remembered himself as a child with ears that stuck out and legs so skinny that friends and relatives believed he had some sort of disease.

Mattie Ashe, Arthur's mother, died shortly before his seventh birthday. Her death occurred at the pitifully young age of twenty-seven and was caused by a stroke brought on by a problem pregnancy and complicated by a weak heart. She had been ill for some time—Arthur later realized that he often envisioned her in a blue corduroy dressing gown. Arthur, Sr., broke the news of his wife's death tearfully to Arthur and his younger brother, Johnnie, as the three sat on the lower bunk in the boys' bedroom.

"Don't cry, Daddy," Arthur told his father. "As long as we have each other, we'll be all right."

The young boy's words were prophetic. His father kept a close eye on Arthur and Johnnie, and the two boys would do well in school and elsewhere. Young Arthur's father was not educated or wealthy, but one of the jobs he held in the city was an important one— he maintained the parks where African Americans were permitted to play. Part of his job was to keep tennis courts in these parks in good playing condition. Shortly after his mother's death, Arthur stood beside one of the courts one morning watching Ron Charity, Richmond's best African-American tennis player.

Charity was practicing his high, hard serves. He could feel the eyes of the thin, silent boy who lived in the only house in leafy, eighteen-acre Brook Field playground. Charity stopped practicing long enough to approach young Arthur and ask, "Would you like to learn to play?" Arthur said he would. "As casually as that, my life was transformed," Arthur would later remember.

Arthur, Sr., felt his son was too thin for football and other contact sports, and he made him take naps long after other children stayed up all day. He was relieved to see the boy learn the rules of tennis as he swatted madly at the bouncing balls. Young Arthur loved the game and showed real ability. A couple of years later, in 1953, the ten-year-old would pose for a newspaper photo amid a number of trophies. But these were trophies won mostly at Brook Field playground, not at the larger and better equipped whites-only private clubs. Except for an occasional white player who wandered onto his local court, Arthur was unable to compete against most of the good players in Richmond.

Many people, in and outside his family, helped young Arthur with his game. But none did more for him than a former college athlete who took up tennis to stay in shape. Robert Walter Johnson was a rugged man, a baseball player, and a college football player in the days when no helmets were worn. He attended several African-American colleges after World War I, eventually earning a medical degree. Johnson settled into his practice in Lynchburg, Virginia, where he spent some time looking for a sport he could play the rest of his life.

"I don't know," she replied.

Ray was uneasy during the examination. The doctor appeared before him as a large blob, and Ray could not make out the features on Dr. McCloud's face.

"Tell me what you can and cannot see," the physician told Ray.

"I used to be able to make out people and trees and cars, things like that," Ray explained. "Big things. Then everything got blurred but I could still make out the different colors, the blues in the sky and the green in the grass. Then even the colors got blurred, but I can still see if it's day or night. I know if it's light or dark."

While Ray was speaking, the doctor looked into his eyes with special lights. Ray felt the heat from the instruments; he imagined looking into the burning sun.

When the examination was over, Dr. McCloud prescribed some ointments and eye drops, hoping that these medications would be of some help. Weeks passed, however, and nothing seemed to aid Ray's condition. Eventually, Dr. McCloud recommended that Mrs. Robinson take her son to a clinic in Madison, not far from Greensville. Mother and son went to the doctor's office in Madison, where Ray was thoroughly examined. Mrs. Robinson turned to the doctor and said, "Tell me, is there hope?"

The doctor paused a long while before he replied. "I'm afraid not, Mrs. Robinson. Your boy is losing his sight."

"But what about cures?" asked Aretha Robinson. "There must be cures."

"I don't know of any," answered the physician, who believed that the blindness was being caused by a disease known as glaucoma.

"I understand," she replied.

Aretha Robinson took Ray by the hand and led him out of the clinic. When they reached Greensville, they walked down the main street of town—past the bank, the post office, the general store, and across the railroad tracks, back into the woods and into their one-room shack. Aretha Robinson had said nothing to her son until they were in the privacy of their home.

"This is not the end of the world," she told Ray. "I'm not saying it's going to be easy, but it's not going to be impossible. You aren't dying. You're losing your sight, not your mind. The rest of your body works fine. Your mind is good, Ray. You can still do whatever you want to do. But I'm going to have to teach you, and you're going to have to pay special attention.

I'm going to teach you to cook and clean and do all your chores like any other child. And the reason I'm going to teach you is 'cause I won't always be around to do for you."

"Don't say that," Ray protested. "You'll always be here."

"No, I won't. You got to know that. And when I'm gone, you're gonna have to do for yourself. Understand?"

Mrs. Robinson reached down and hugged her son with all the strength of her frail body. She kissed his forehead and said, "I love you and I'm going to help you. I'm going to help you do for yourself."

A week later, on a Saturday morning, a woman named Mary Jane came to visit. Mary Jane was Aretha Robinson's age and once had been married to Bailey, Ray's father. Over the years she had grown especially fond of Ray. In fact, the two were so close that, although he called Aretha "Mama," he referred to Mary Jane as "Mother."

Ray responded to Mary Jane's knock on the door. He had a scrub brush in his hand when she entered the shack and she saw how his eyes were squeezed together, closed tight. "What in the world are you doing?" she asked.

"Scrubbing the floor, like Mama showed me," answered Ray.

"Your mama shouldn't be making you do stuff like that," said Mary Jane, handing Ray several pieces of his favorite chocolate.

"Why not?" asked Mrs. Robinson, who had just arrived from town. The two women were friendly but differed greatly when it came to raising Ray. Aretha Robinson was a strict disciplinarian, whereas Mary Jane was extremely lenient. In different ways and for different reasons, Ray loved both women.

"Everyone's talkin' 'bout how you are treating this boy like he can see," said Mary Jane.

"Not seeing don't keep him from playing the piano, does it?" Aretha asked.

"I love playing the piano," Ray interjected.

"But he shouldn't be . . ." Mary Jane started to argue.

"He should be doing what most other kids are doing because he's as smart and strong as any of them," Aretha tersely replied.

"Look, 'Retha," Mary Jane tried to explain, "I know about strong. I'm working over at the sawmill right beside all those men, doing the same heavy hauling as them. But being blind is different."

Sojourner Truth

PETER KRASS

> In her mid-forties, Truth began her crusade as a traveling preacher. Asking God to give her a new name to use as she went about doing His work, she received a message to change her slave name of Isabella to Sojourner Truth.

When the first bit of sunlight illuminated the sky over New York City on June 1, 1843, Isabella was already awake, stuffing a few dresses into an old pillowcase. The day of her departure had come at last. Her employers, the Whitings, were stunned by the news that she was leaving and asked her where she would be staying. "The Lord is going to give me a new home," Isabella told them.

Heading east, in the direction that an inner voice had told her to follow, Isabella took a ferry to Brooklyn. There she disembarked and began walking on a road that stretched eastward, toward Long Island. At age 46, she felt free, as though she were repeating the escape from slavery that she had made nearly 17 years before.

However, something still bothered Isabella. She believed that the name she had been given as a slave was inappropriate for a person who was beginning a new life as God's pilgrim. She wanted a new name, a free woman's name.

Calling on God for help in choosing her new name, Isabella received an answer. She should call herself "Sojourner." She thought that it was a good name for someone who had been called on, she later said, to "travel up and down the land, showing the people their sins, and being a sign unto them." The name also reminded her of the holy people described in the Bible who had traveled to foreign lands to preach the word of God. More and more, she felt as though she was following in the tradition of the great prophets of biblical times.

Proudly bearing her new name, Sojourner continued walking for another few miles, until she saw a woman working in front of a house. Having grown thirsty, Sojourner asked her for some water. As the woman was gladly fulfilling Sojourner's request, she asked the traveler what her name was.

When Sojourner told her, the woman attempted to find out what Sojourner's last name was and asked, "Sojourner what?" Her name was simply Sojourner, the traveler

said, and then she continued on her journey. Yet the woman's question continued to nag at her. Why did she not have a last name?

Once again, Sojourner prayed for guidance. And once more, an answer came to her: Truth. Her full name would be Sojourner Truth—a very suitable name for one of God's pilgrims, she thought.

As Truth traveled east across Long Island the white farmers whom she encountered stopped their work to listen to her, finding themselves enthralled by the powerful and inspiring manner in which she spoke. They were amazed that she seemed to know every word in the Bible even though she was illiterate.

Word about the fiery preacher spread throughout Long Island. People began to whisper, "It must be Sojourner Truth" whenever she appeared at a religious meeting in a new neighborhood.

Eventually, Truth decided that she should follow God's call by heading to another area. She took a ship across Long Island Sound and proceeded northward, preaching in Connecticut and Massachusetts. Wherever she went, people flocked to listen to her.

Truth eventually arrived in Northampton, a town located along the Connecticut River in the heart of Massachusetts. There she visited the Northampton Association of Education and Industry, a cooperative community that operated a silkworm farm. The community members shared equally in all of the work but did not participate in any of the religious fanaticism that had existed in Robert Matthew's Kingdom commune. Attracted by the Northampton Association's idealism and spirit of good fellowship, Truth joined the community in late 1843.

While Truth was living at the community, she met many prominent public figures. Among the people who either lived in the community or came to visit the Northampton Association were abolitionists Samuel Hill, George Benson, and David Ruggles, as well as two of the leading organizers and speakers of the antislavery movement, William Lloyd Garrison and Frederick Douglass. Although the importation of slaves into the United States was forbidden after 1801, slavery was still being practiced in most of the southern states. Led by Garrison and Douglass, the abolitionist movement sought to put an end to slavery.

In 1831, Garrison had founded an influential antislavery newspaper, the Liberator, and he had formed the New England Anti-Slavery Society during the following year.

Douglass, who had escaped from slavery in 1838, was just beginning to enjoy his reputation as one of the most eloquent abolitionist lecturers. Truth was greatly impressed by the effectiveness of these activists in stirring up antislavery sentiment in the North.

Between 1846 and 1850, Truth became increasingly involved in the antislavery crusade. For the most part, Truth associated more with Garrison's American Anti-Slavery Society than with its rival organization, the less militant American and Foreign Anti-Slavery Society.

Garrison's organization distrusted political parties and stated that slavery could be destroyed only by moral persuasion. The Garrisonians believed that accounts of the cruelties of the slave system printed in abolitionist newspapers would eventually compel the slaveholders to change their ways. The American and Foreign Anti-Slavery Society, on the other hand, cooperated with the Liberty party, the Free Soil party, and other progressive political organizations in working for national laws that would outlaw slavery. . . .

By the early 1850s, many slave narratives had caught the public's attention. The most widely read of these books was The Narrative of Frederick Douglass, which was published in 1845, at a time when the abolitionist leader was still a fugitive slave. These books not only presented the unvarnished truth about the brutal salve system, but they also gave stirring accounts of the courage and dignity of slaves who had escaped from bondage. Some of the slave narratives became best-sellers, and they helped to arouse a growing feeling of moral revulsion against slavery among Northerners.

Olive Gilbert, a friend of Truth, believed that a narrative of her early life as a slave in the North and her profound faith in God would be uplifting to many people. Truth liked the idea, and in 1850, she and Gilbert published The Narrative of Sojourner Truth, which included an introduction by Garrison. Truth, who could not read the account of her own life, was able to support herself by selling copies of the book at abolitionist meetings.

The fight against slavery was not the only cause to which Truth was attracted. During her stay at the Northampton Association, she had heard lecturers who advocated that women be given the same political and legal rights enjoyed by men. Recognizing that she and the women's rights speakers were kindred spirits, Truth decided to join their ranks in yet another battle for freedom.

Not all of the male members of the antislavery movement agreed with Truth and the other women abolitionists on the issue of women's equality. Garrison and Douglass were avid supporters of women's rights, but many of the abolitionists remained unsympathetic to the feminist cause and did not want to allow women to assume leadership roles in anti-slavery societies . . .

. . . In 1848, feminists organized the first national women's rights conference at a church in Seneca Falls, New York. Hundreds of female activists were joined by a courageous group of men who supported women's equality. Disregarding the jeers of antifeminist men in the audience, the delegates issued a Declaration of Sentiments and Resolutions, a document based to a great extent on the Declaration of Independence. The declaration proposed an 11-point plan for helping women achieve equality with men.

Truth did not attend the 1848 convention, but she went to many other women's rights meetings. In October 1850, she traveled to Worcester, Massachusetts, to speak at that year's national women's rights convention.

At last, Truth was called on to speak. "Sisters," she began, "I ain't clear what you'd be after. If women want any rights more than they's got, why don't they just take them, and not be talking about it?"

However, the problem of attaining equal rights for women was more complex than Truth was willing to admit at the convention. The chief problem was that a sizable number of men strongly opposed equality for women and were ready to fight to preserve the status quo. In addition, the women's rights activists disagreed among themselves about the best way to achieve their goals. Some wanted to pursue their rights in law courts, while others believed that putting pressure on political parties and congressmen would achieve better results. The debates would continue for years at annual conventions held throughout the country.

Yet Truth's defiant message at the 1850 women's rights convention heartened the ranks of the nation's abolitionists and feminists as well as all of the oppressed people who yearned for equality. "Why not just take your rights?" she had asked. Many Americans who were deprived of their rights in their own land were beginning to ask the same question.

Slavery

Incidents in the Life of a Slave Girl

HARRIET A. JACOBS

Harriet Jacobs was a slave for twenty-seven years before escaping to freedom in the North. Her autobiography vividly documents the evils of slavery as well as her own ability to maintain her spirit and dignity.

CHILDHOOD

I was born a slave but never knew it till six years of happy childhood had passed away. My father was a carpenter and considered so intelligent and skillful in his trade, that, when buildings out of the common line were to be erected, he was sent for from long distances, to be head workman.

On condition of paying his mistress two hundred dollars a year, and supporting himself, he was allowed to work at his trade, and manage his own affairs. His strongest wish was to purchase his children, but though he several times offered his hard earnings for that purpose, he never succeeded.

In complexion my parents were a light shade of brownish yellow, and were termed mulattos. They lived together in a comfortable home; and, though we were all slaves, I was so fondly shielded that I never dreamed I was a piece of merchandise, trusted to them for safekeeping, and liable to be demanded of them at any moment.

I had one brother, William, who was two years younger than myself—a bright, affectionate child. I had also a great treasure in my maternal grandmother, who was a remarkable woman in many respects. She was the daughter of a planter in South Carolina, who, at his death, left her mother and his three children free, with money to go to St. Augustine, where they had relatives. It was during the Revolutionary War; and they were captured on their passage, carried back, and sold to different purchasers.

Such was the story my grandmother used to tell me; but I do not remember all the particulars. She was a little girl when she was captured and sold to the keeper of a large hotel. I have often heard her tell how hard she fared during childhood. But as she grew older, she evinced so much intelligence, and was so faithful, that her master and mistress could not help seeing it was for their interest to take care of such a valuable piece of property.

She became an indispensable person in the household, officiating in all capacities, from cook and wet nurse to seamstress. She was much praised for her cooking; and her nice crackers became so famous in the neighborhood that many people were desirous of obtaining them. In consequence of numerous requests of this kind, she asked permission of her mistress to bake crackers at night, after all the household work was done; and she obtained leave to do it, provided she would clothe herself and her children from the profits.

Upon these terms, after working hard all day for her mistress, she began her midnight bakings, assisted by her two oldest children. The business proved profitable; and each year she laid by a little, which was saved for a fund to purchase her children. Her master died, and the property was divided among his heirs. The widow had her dower in the hotel, which she continued to keep open. My grandmother remained in her service as a slave; but her children were divided among her master's children. As she had five, Benjamin, the youngest one, was sold, in order that each heir might have an equal portion of dollars and cents.

There was so little difference in our ages that Benjamin seemed more like my brother than my uncle. He was a bright, handsome lad, nearly white; for he inherited the complexion my grandmother had derived from Anglo-Saxon ancestors. Though only ten years old, seven hundred and twenty dollars was paid for him. His sale was a terrible blow to my grandmother; but she was naturally hopeful and she went to work with renewed energy, trusting in time to be able to purchase some of her children.

She had laid up three hundred dollars, which her mistress one day begged as a loan, promising to pay her soon. The reader probably knows that no promise or writing given to a slave is legally binding; for, according to Southern laws, a slave, being property, can hold no property. When my grandmother lent her hard saved earnings to her mistress, she trusted solely to her honor. The honor of a slaveholder to a slave!

To this good grandmother I was indebted for many comforts. My brother Willie and I often received portions of the crackers, cakes, and preserves she made to sell; and after we ceased to be children we were indebted to her for many more important services.

Such were the unusually fortunate circumstances of my early childhood. When I was six years old, my mother died; and then, for the first time, I learned, by the talk around me, that I was a slave.

My mother's mistress was the daughter of my grandmother's mistress. She was the foster sister of my mother. They were both nourished at my grandmother's breast. In fact, my mother had been weaned at three months old, that the babe of the mistress might obtain sufficient food. They played together as children; and, when they became women, my mother was a most faithful servant to her white foster sister. On my mother's death-bed her mistress promised that her children should never suffer for any thing; and during her lifetime she kept her word.

They all spoke kindly of my dead mother, who had been a slave merely in name, but in nature was noble and womanly. I grieved for her and my young mind was troubled with the thought who would now take care of me and my little brother. I was told that my home was now to be with my mistress; and I found it a happy one. No toilsome or disagreeable duties were imposed upon me. My mistress was so kind to me that I was always glad to do her bidding, and proud to labor for her as much as my young years would permit.

I would sit by her side for hours, sewing diligently, with a heart as free from care as that of any free-born white child. When she thought I was tired, she would send me out to run and jump; and away I bounded, to gather berries or flowers to decorate her room. Those were happy days—too happy to last. The slave child had no thought for the morrow; but there came that blight, which too surely waits every human being born to be a chattel.

When I was nearly twelve years old, my kind mistress sickened and died. As I saw the cheek grow paler, and the eye more glassy, how earnestly I prayed in my heart that she might live! I loved her; for she had been almost like a mother to me. My prayers were not answered. She died, and they buried her in the little churchyard, where, day after day, my tears fell upon her grave.

I was sent to spend a week with my grandmother. I was now old enough to begin to think of the future; and again and again I asked myself what they would do with me. I felt sure I should never find another mistress so kind as the one who was gone. She had promised my dying mother that her children should never suffer for any thing; and when I remembered that, and recalled her many proofs of attachment to me, I could not help having some hopes that she had left me free. My friends were almost certain it would be so. They thought she would be sure to do it, on account of my mother's love and faithful service. But, alas! we all know that the memory of a faithful slave does not avail much to save her children from the auction block.

After a brief period of suspense, the will of my mistress was read, and we learned that she had bequeathed me to her sister's daughter, a child of five years old. So vanished our hopes. My mistress had taught me the precepts of God's word: "Thou shalt love thy neighbor as thyself." "Whatsoever ye would that men should do unto you, do ye even so unto them." But I was her slave, and I suppose she did not recognize me as her neighbor.

I would do much to blot out from my memory that one great wrong. As a child, I loved my mistress; and, looking back on the happy days I spent with her, I try to think with less bitterness of this act of injustice. While I was with her, she taught me to read and spell; and for this privilege, which so rarely falls to the lot of a slave, I bless her memory.

She possessed but few slaves; and at her death those were all distributed among her relatives. Five of them were my grandmother's children, and had shared the same milk that nourished her mother's children. Notwithstanding my grandmother's long and faithful service to her owners, not one of their children escaped the auction block.

These God-breathing machines are no more, in the sight of their masters, than the cotton they plant, or the horses they tend.

Up from Slavery

BOOKER T. WASHINGTON

Booker T. Washington was approximately six years old when the Civil War ended and all slaves were declared free. His stepfather had already found his way to the little town of Malden in the Kanawha Valley in the new state of West Virginia. He got a job in a salt-furnace and sent for the rest of the family.

BOYHOOD DAYS

From the time I can remember having any thoughts about anything, I can recall that I had an intense longing to learn to read. I determined that, while quite a small child, that if I accomplished nothing else in life, I would in some way get enough education to enable me to read common books and newspapers. Soon after we got settled in some manner in our new cabin in West Virginia, I induced my mother to get hold of a book for me. How or where she got it, I do not know, but in some way she procured an old copy of Webster's "blue-back" spelling book, which contained the alphabet, followed by such meaningless words as "ab," "ba," "ca," "da."

I began at once to devour this book. I think that it was the first one I ever had in my hands. I had learned from somebody that the way to begin to read was to learn the alphabet, so I tried in all the ways I could think of to learn it—all, of course, without a teacher, for I could find no one to teach me. At that time there was not a single member of my race anywhere near us who could read, and I was too timid to approach any of the white people.

In some way, within a few weeks, I mastered the greater portion of the alphabet. In all my efforts to learn to read my mother shared fully my ambition, and sympathized with me, and aided me in every way that she could. Though she was totally ignorant, so far as mere book knowledge was concerned, she had high ambitions for her children, and a large fund of good, hard, common sense which seemed to enable her to meet and master every situation. If I have done anything in life worth attention, I feel sure that I inherited the disposition to do so from my mother.

In the midst of my struggles and longing for an education, a young colored boy who had learned to read in the state of Ohio came to Malden. As soon as the colored people found out that the boy could read, a newspaper was secured, and at the close of work every day this young man would be surrounded by a group of men and women who were anxious to hear him read the news contained in the papers. How I used to envy this man! He seemed to me to be the one man in all the world who ought to be satisfied with his attainments.

About this time the question of having some kind of school opened for the colored children in the village began to be discussed. As it would be the first school for Negro children that had ever been opened in Virginia, it was, of course, to be a great event, and the discussion excited the widest interest. The most perplexing question was where to find a teacher. The young man from Ohio who had learned to read the papers was considered, but his age was against him. In the midst of the discussion about a teacher, another young colored man from Ohio, who had been a soldier, found his way into town. It was soon learned that he possessed considerable education, and he was engaged by the colored people to teach their first school.

As yet no free schools had been started for colored people in that section, hence each family agreed to pay a certain amount each month, with the understanding that the teacher was to "board 'round"—that is, spend a day with each student's family. This was not bad for the teacher, for each family tried to provide the very best on the day he was to be their guest. I recall that I looked forward with an anxious appetite to the "teacher's day" at our little cabin.

This experience of a whole race beginning to go to school for the first time presents one of the most interesting studies that has ever occurred in connection with the development of any race. Few people who were not right in the midst of the scenes can form any exact idea of the intense desire which the people of my race showed for an education. Few were too young, and none too old, to make the attempt to learn. As fast as any kind of teachers could be secured, not only were day-schools filled, but night-schools as well. The great ambition of the older people was to try to learn to read the Bible before they died.

With this end in view, men and women who were fifty or seventy-five years old would often be found in the night-school. Sunday schools were formed soon after freedom, but the principal book studied in the Sunday school was the spelling book.

The opening of the school in the Kanawha Valley, however, brought to me one of the keenest disappointments that I ever experienced. I had been working in a salt-furnace for several months, and my stepfather had discovered that I had financial value, and so, when the school opened, he decided that he could not spare me from my work. The disappointment was made all the more severe by reason of the fact that my place of work was where I could see the happy children passing to and from school, mornings and afternoons. Despite this disappointment, however, I determined that I would learn something, anyway. I applied myself with greater earnestness than ever to the mastering of what was in the "blue-back" speller.

My mother sympathized with me and sought to comfort me in all the ways she could, and to help me to find a way to learn. After a while I succeeded in making arrangements with the teacher to give me some lessons at night, after the day's work was done. These night lessons were so welcome that I think I learned more at night than the other children did during the day; but my boyish heart was still set upon going to the day school, and I let no opportunity slip to push my case. Finally I won, and was permitted to go to the school in the day for a few months, with the understanding that I was to rise early in the morning and work in the furnace till nine o'clock, and return immediately after school closed in the afternoon for at least two more hours of work.

The schoolhouse was some distance from the furnace, and as I had to work till nine o'clock, and the school opened at nine, I found myself in a difficulty. To get around this difficulty I yielded to a temptation for which most people, I suppose, will condemn me; but since it is a fact, I might as well state it. There was a large clock in a little office in the furnace. This clock, of course, all the hundred or more workmen depended upon to regulate their hours of beginning and ending the day's work. I got the idea that the way for me to reach school on time was to move the clock hands from half-past eight up to the nine o'clock mark. This I found myself doing morning after morning, till the furnace "boss" discovered that something was wrong, and locked the clock in a case. I did not mean to inconvenience anybody. I simply meant to reach school on time.

When, however, I found myself at the school for the first time, I was confronted with two other difficulties. In the first place, I saw that all of the other children wore hats or caps on their heads, and I had neither hat nor cap. In fact, I do not remember that up to the time of going to school I had ever worn any kind of covering upon my head, nor do I recall that either I or anybody else had even thought anything about the need of covering for my head. But of course when I saw how all the other boys were dressed, I began to feel quite uncomfortable.

As usual, I put the case before my mother, and she explained to me that she had no money with which to buy a "store hat." This was a rather new institution at that time among the members of my race, and was considered quite the thing for young and old to own, but that she would find a way to help me out of the difficulty. Accordingly, she got two pieces of "homespun" and sewed them together, and I was soon the proud possessor of my first cap.

The lesson that my mother taught me in this has always remained with me, and I have tried as best I could to teach it to others. I have always felt proud, whenever I think of the incident, that my mother had strength of character enough not to be led into the temptation of seeming to be that which she was not—of trying to impress my schoolmates and others with the fact that she was able to buy me a "store hat" when she was not.

My second difficulty was with regard to my name, or rather a name. From the time when I could remember, I had been called simply "Booker." Before going to school it had never occurred to me that it was needful to have an additional name. But when I heard the school roll called, I noticed that all of the children had at least two names, and some of them indulged in what seemed to me the extravagance of having three. By the time the occasion came for the enrolling of my name, an idea occurred to me; and so when the teacher asked me what my full name was, I calmly told him "Booker Washington," as if I had been called by that name all of my life—and by that name I have since been known.

Later in my life I found that my mother had given me the name of "Booker Taliaferro" soon after I was born, but in some way that part of my name seemed to disappear, and for a long while was forgotten; but as soon as I found out about it, I revived it. I think there are not many men in our country who have had the privilege of naming themselves in the way that I have.

Narrative of the Life of Frederick Douglass, an American Slave

Frederick Douglass was born Frederick Augustus Washington Bailey in 1818. When he was seven years old he was sold to Hugh Auld in Baltimore, Maryland. Douglass, who changed his name after escaping from slavery, was a brilliant writer and speaker, a great leader, and the most important black abolitionist of the nineteenth century. The following passages are from his autobiography.

CHAPTER VII

I lived in Master Hugh's family about seven years. During this time, I succeeded in learning to read and write. In accomplishing this, I was compelled to resort to various stratagems. I had no regular teacher. My mistress, who had kindly commenced to instruct me, had, in compliance with the advice and direction of her husband, not only ceased to instruct, but had set her face against my being instructed by anyone else.

It is due, however, to my mistress to say of her that she did not adopt this course of treatment immediately. She at first lacked the depravity indispensable to shutting me up in mental darkness. It was at least necessary for her to have some training in the exercise of irresponsible power, to make her equal to the task of treating me as though I were a brute.

My mistress was a kind and tender-hearted woman, and in the simplicity of her soul she commenced, when I first went to live with her, to treat me as she supposed one human being ought to treat another. In entering upon the duties of a slaveholder, she did not seem to perceive that I sustained to her the relation of a mere chattel, and that for her to treat me as a human being was not only wrong, but dangerously so. Slavery proved as injurious to her as it did to me.

When I went there, she was a pious, warm, and tender-hearted woman. There was no sorrow or suffering for which she had not a tear. She had bread for the hungry, clothes for the naked, and comfort for every mourner that came within her reach. Slavery soon proved its ability to divest her of these heavenly qualities. Under its influence, the tender heart became stone, and the lamb-like disposition gave way to one of tiger-like fierceness.

The first step in her downward course was in her ceasing to instruct me. She now commenced to practice her husband's precepts. She finally became even more violent in her opposition than her husband himself. She was not satisfied in simply doing as well as he had commanded—she seemed anxious to do better. Nothing seemed to make her more angry than to see me with a newspaper. She seemed to think that here lay the danger. I have had her rush at me with a face made all up of fury, and snatch from me a newspaper, in a manner that fully revealed her apprehension. She was an apt woman, and a little experience soon demonstrated, to her satisfaction, that education and slavery were incompatible with each other.

From this time I was most narrowly watched. If I was in a separate room any considerable length of time, I was sure to be suspected of having a book, and was at once called to give an account of myself. All this, however, was too late. The first step had been taken. Mistress, in teaching me the alphabet, had given me the "inch," and no precaution could prevent me from taking the "ell."

The plan I adopted, and the one by which I was most successful, was that of making friends of all the little white boys whom I met in the street. As many of these as I could, I converted into teachers. With their kindly aid, obtained at different times and in different

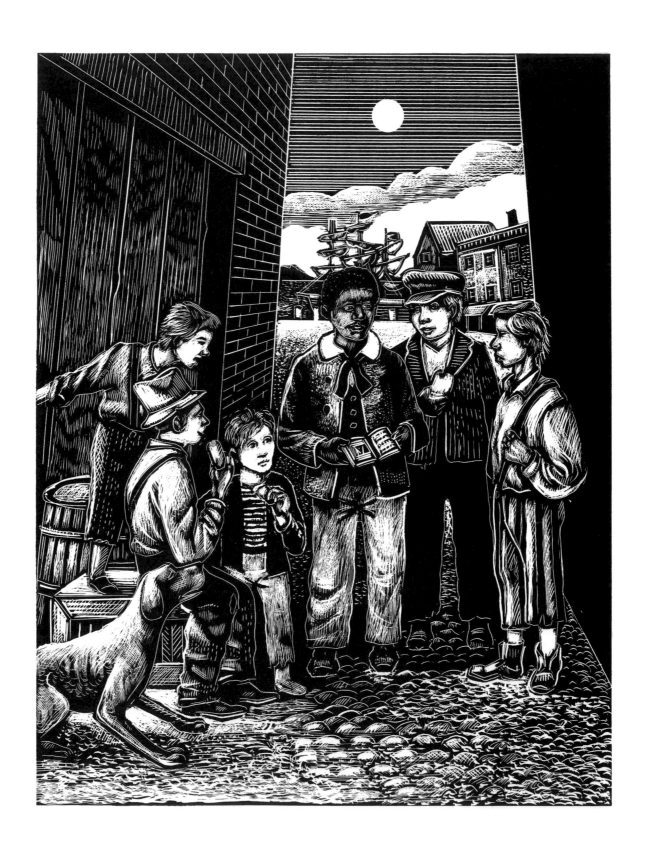

places, I finally succeeded in learning to read. When I was sent on errands, I always took my book with me, and by going one part of my errand quickly, I found time to get a lesson before my return.

I used always to carry bread with me, enough of which was always in the house, and to which I was always welcome; for I was much better off in this regard than many of the poor white children in our neighborhood. This bread I used to bestow upon the hungry little urchins, who, in return, would give me that more valuable bread of knowledge. I am strongly tempted to give the names of two or three of those little boys, as a testimonial of the gratitude and affection I bear them. But prudence forbids—not that it would injure me, but it might embarrass them; for it is almost an unpardonable offense to teach slaves to read in this Christian country.

It is enough to say of the dear little fellows, that they lived on Philpot Street, very near Durgin and Bailey's shipyard. I used to talk this matter of slavery over with them. I would sometimes say to them, I wished I could be as free as they would be when they got to be men. "You will be free as soon as you are twenty-one, *but I am a slave for life!* Have not I as good a right to be free as you have?" These words used to trouble them; they would express for me the liveliest sympathy, and console me with the hope that something would occur by which I might be free.

I was now about twelve years old, and the thought of being a slave for life began to bear heavily upon my heart. Just about this time, I got hold of a book entitled "The Columbian Orator." Every opportunity I got, I used to read this book. I found in it a dialogue between a master and his slave. The slave was represented as having run away from his master three times. The dialogue represented the conversation which took place between them, when the slave was retaken the third time. In this dialogue, the whole argument in behalf of slavery was brought forward by the master, all of which was disposed of by the slave. The slave was made to say some very smart as well as impressive things in reply to his master—things which had the desired though unexpected effect—for the conversation resulted in the voluntary emancipation of the slave on the part of the master.

In the same book, I met with one of Sheridan's mighty speeches on and in behalf of Catholic emancipation. These were choice documents to me. I read them over and over again with unabated interest. The moral which I gained from the dialogue was the power of truth over the conscience of even a slaveholder. What I got from Sheridan was a bold denunciation of slavery, and a powerful vindication of human rights.

Every little while, I could hear something about the abolitionists. It was some time before I found what the word meant. It was always used in such connections as to make it an interesting word to me. If a slave ran away and succeeded in getting clear, or if a slave killed his master, set fire to a barn, or did any thing very wrong in the mind of a slave-holder, it was spoken of as the fruit of "abolition." Hearing the word in this connection very often, I set about learning what it meant. The dictionary afforded me no help. I found it was "the act of abolishing" but then I did not know what was to be abolished. Here I was perplexed. I did not dare to ask any one about its meaning, for I was satisfied that it was something they wanted me to know very little about.

After a patient waiting, I got one of our city papers, containing an account of the number of petitions from the north, praying for the abolition of slavery in the District of Columbia, and of the slave trade between the States. From this time I understood the word "abolition" and "abolitionist," and always drew near when that word was spoken, expecting to hear something of importance to myself and fellow-slaves.

The light broke in upon me by degrees. I went one day down on the wharf of Mr. Waters; and seeing two Irishmen unloading a scow of stone, I went, unasked, and helped them. When we had finished, one of them came to me and asked me if I were a slave. I told him I was. He asked, "Are ye a slave for life?" I told him that I was. The good Irishman seemed to be deeply affected by the statement. He said to the other that it was a pity so fine a little fellow as myself should be a slave for life. They both advised me to run away to the north; that I should find friends there, and that I should be free. I pretended not to be interested in what they said and treated them as if I did not understand them; for I feared they might be treacherous. White men have been known to encourage slaves to escape, and then, to get the reward, catch them and return them to their masters. I was afraid that these seemingly good men might use me so. But I remembered their advice, and from that time resolved to run away. I was too young to think of doing it immediately; besides, I wished to learn how to write, as I might have occasion to write my own pass. I consoled myself with the hope that I should one day find a good chance. Meanwhile, I would learn to write.

How I might learn to write was suggested to me by being in Durgin and Bailey's shipyard, and seeing the carpenter, after getting a piece of timber ready for use, write on the timber the name of that part of the ship for which it was intended. When a piece was intended for the larboard side, it would be marked "L." For the starboard side, it would be marked "S." A piece for the larboard side forward, would be marked "L.F.," and for the starboard aft, it would be marked "S.A." I soon learned the names of these letters, and for what they were intended. I immediately commenced copying them, and in a short time was able to make the four letters named.

After that, when I met with any boy who I knew could write, I would tell him I could write as well as he. The next word would be, "I don't believe you. Let me see you try it." I would then make the letters I had been so fortunate to learn, and ask him to beat that. In this way I got a good many lessons in writing, which it is quite possible I should never have gotten in any other way.

During this time, my copy book was the board fence, brick wall, and pavement. My pen and ink was a lump of chalk. With these, I learned mainly how to write. I then commenced and continued copying the Italics in "Webster's Spelling Book," until I could make them all without looking at the book. By this time, my little Master Thomas had gone to school, and learned how to write, and had written over a number of copy books. These had been brought home and then laid aside. My mistress used to go to class meetings at the Wilk Street meetinghouse every Monday afternoon, and leave me to take care of the house. When left thus, I used to spend the time in writing in the spaces left in Master Thomas's copy book, copying what he had written. I continued to do this until I could write what he had written. Thus, after a long, tedious effort for years, I finally succeeded in learning how to write.

African-American Songs

African music came to America with the slaves. Tribal history, culture, and religious beliefs had always been passed through song and dance from one generation to the next. On the plantations, blacks developed their own musical tradition. The coded language of their spiritual songs provided a way for slaves to secretly communicate. "Heaven" and the "promised land" referred to the joy of freedom, "crossing the River Jordan" was a metaphor for crossing the Ohio and Mississippi into abolitionist territory, and references to trains were reminders of the Underground Railroad.

Miss Mary Mack

TRADITIONAL/HAND-CLAPPING SONG

When not working in the fields, hand-clapping songs were sung
by enslaved African-American children to amuse themselves.

Miss Mary Mack, Mack, Mack,
All dressed in black, black, black,
With silver buttons, buttons, buttons,
All down her back, back, back.

She asked her mother, mother, mother,
For fifteen cents, cents, cents,
To see the elephant, elephant, elephant,
Jump over the fence, fence, fence.

He jumped so high, high, high,
He almost reached the sky, sky, sky,
And he didn't come back, back, back,
Until the Fourth of July, 'ly, 'ly.

About the Illustrators

CHRISTIAN CLAYTON was born in Colorado, 1967. He graduated in 1991 from Art Center College of Design in Pasadena, California receiving a B.F.A. He has had numerous solo and group exhibitions in major U.S. cities. His artwork has been featured in national and international print and media. He currently teaches and lectures at The Art Center College of Design. He also collaborates with his brother Rob Clayton to produce dynamic images sought after for commercial use as well as by private collectors. In tandem, they are known as The Clayton Brothers. They live and work in Los Angeles, California. www.claytonbrothers.com

JAN SPIVEY GILCHRIST'S illustrations have graced the pages of the Coretta Scott King Award book *Nathaniel Talking*, Coretta Scott King Honor book *Night On Neighborhood Street*, and *For the Love of the Game*, a Young Hoosier Award nominee, all three by Eloise Greenfield. She has illustrated over fifty children's books and is the author of *Indigo, Moonlight Gold* and *Mandelia*. She lives in suburban Chicago with her husband Dr. Kelvin Gilchrist and her son William Kelvin.

CHRISTY HALE has illustrated numerous books for children, including the award winning Elizabeti series published by Lee & Low Books. Hale also works as art director and book designer for children's books, and has been an art educator for all ages of children as well as adults. After 18 years in New York, Christy has recently relocated to northern California with her husband and their daughter.

MICHAEL McCURDY is the illustrator of almost 200 highly acclaimed books, for both adults and children. He has also written a dozen books, and received several *Parents' Choice* awards, and a number of CBC-NCSS Notable Trade Book in the Field of Social Studies awards. He has also twice received the *New York Times* Ten Best Illustrated Books Award. He lives in the Berkshire Hills of Massachusetts. Learn more about Michael McCurdy at www.michaelmccurdy.com

Acknowledgments

From AFRICAN WONDER TALES by Frances Carpenter Huntington, copyright © 1963 by Frances Carpenter Huntington. Used by permission of Doubleday, a division of Random House, Inc.

From ARTHUR ASHE by David K. Wright. Used with permission by Enslow Publishers, Inc., Springfield, New jersey. Copyright © 1996 by David K. Wright.

From RAY CHARLES by David Ritz. Copyright © 2003 by Chelsea House Publishers, a subsidiary of Haights Cross Communications.